Universal Responsibility
and
The Good Heart

Universal Responsibility and The Good Heart

by
Bhikshu Tenzin Gyatso,
the Fourteenth Dalai Lama

LIBRARY OF TIBETAN WORKS AND ARCHIVES

ISBN: 81-85102-45-7

Published by the Library of Tibetan Works & Archives, Dharamsala, Dist. Kangra, H.P. (India), and printed at Indraprastha Press (C.B.T.), Nehru House, 4, Bahadur Shah Zafar Marg, New Delhi 110002.

Contents

Publisher's Note

In 1975 the Library of Tibetan Works and Archives published a small booklet of edited materials from the talks and discussions given by His Holiness the Dalai Lama during his first tour of Europe a year and a half earlier. Entitled *Universal Responsibility and the Good Heart*, this work was very well received and was republished in whole and in part by a number of magazines and journals around the world.

When the time came to bring out a second edition of this booklet, it was suggested that the text should be expanded upon with other material by His Holiness that had come out over the past few years but that had as yet not appeared in book form. The work of collecting and preparing this larger text was assigned to K. Dhondup and Glenn H. Mullin, two members of our Research and Translation Bureau. Following the success and warm reception of that collection, it was decided that the third edition should be augmented with further material. Thus, a number of interviews, talks and articles by His Holiness, which have appeared since 1980, have been incorporated, in whole or in part, into the collection under the same themes and headings as before. This work was done by Tsepak Rigzin and Jeremy Russell, also members of our Research and Translation Bureau.

It was decided to arrange the collection according to four themes: His Holiness' relationship with the Tibetan peoples; his manner of dealing with the non-Buddhists who come to him for advice; his teachings to the international Buddhist community; and his views and sense of political responsibility as regards Tibet in particular and the world situation in general.

Chapter I, therefore, comprises an extract from a speech given (in Tibetan) by His Holiness to a large group of refugees at the Tibetan Refugee Camp in Delhi in 1963. Translated and edited by Lobsang Chophel with G.H. Mullin, it represents the direct and personal nature with which His Holiness communicates with his people, and conveys the flavour of his religious and secular advice to them. Some of the ideas in this article are clarified with extracts from a talk His Holiness gave to the Tibetans a few years later that touched upon similar ground.

Chapter II, a reprint of *Universal Responsibility and the Good Heart*, reflects the ecumenical spirit with which His Holiness teaches non-Buddhists who ask him for guidance. The textual matter in this section is collected from a number of talks, TV appearances, press interviews and so forth given by His Holiness during his first tour of Europe in 1973. His Holiness spoke exclusively in English during this tour, and the language has been left much as he spoke it in order to retain the atmosphere of the original. It was edited into its present form mainly by Mrs. Joyce Murdoch. Additions to the Questions and Answers in this Chapter under the headings 'The Future', 'Nuclear War' and 'Social Action' have been taken from interviews with His Holiness which appeared in the *Washington Times* in September 1984 and the *East West Journal* of February 1984. Part Three, 'Kindness—a Simple Religion for Mankind' was taken from a talk His Holiness gave in English to a mixed audience in Gangtok, Sikkim in October 1981.

Chapter III, a collection of minor writings prepared for various Buddhist groups over the past two decades, reveals the clarity and precision with which His Holiness treats the profound subjects of the Buddhadharma.

Parts One, Three, Five, Seven and Nine of this chapter are reprinted from the booklet *Short Essays on Buddhist Thought and Practice* (Secretariat of H.H. the Dalai Lama, Dharamsala, 1966). Part Two, 'Happiness, Karma and the Mind', first appeared in the Tibet *Society Occasional Paper* No. 1 (Indiana, U.S.A., Dec. 1969). I myself had the pleasure of translating all of the above essays in the late 1960s while working as an aide to His Holiness. Part Three was originally written for the International Buddhist Conference in Japan in 1978, and Part Ten for the International Buddhist Conference in New Delhi in 1978. Both of these were translated by Dr. Lobsang Rabgay. Part Six was derived from the advice introducing and concluding an explanation of a Bhikshu's vows; translated and compiled by Tsepak Rigzin and Glenn H. Mullin, it first appeared in *Tibetan Review* (Sept. 1982). The material for the questions and answers in Part Eleven was largely collected from three sources: 'When the Iron Bird Flies', an interview by Michael Hellbach translated by Sharpa Tulku (*From Tushita*, No.1, Germany 1977); 'Answers to Questions' by H.H. the Dalai Lama (*The American Theosophist*, Spring 1977); and 'We change our body from time to time' by Graham Coleman (*Tibetan Review*, Nov. 1981).

Part One of Chapter IV first appeared in *Leader's Magazine*, New York (May 1979) under the title 'Place of Ethics and Morality in Politics'. Part Two is reprinted from *The Tibet Journal*, Vol 5, Nos.1 & 2. Part Three, translated by Tsering Wangyal, originally appeared in *The Asian*

Wall Street Journal, Hong Kong on Aug. 25 1977 as 'The Dalai Lama Speaks out His Mind'. Part Four was also first published by *The Asian Wall Street Journal*, (No. 8, 1979) and carried the same title as it does here. Part Five, 'Spiritual Contributiôns to Social Progress', first appeared in the *Wall Street Journal* (New York, Oct. 1981). Part Six, 'Meeting Points in Science and Spirituality' is an address originally delivered to the 'Other Realities' Conference organised by Forum International at Alpbach in Austria in September 1983. The questions and answers in Part Seven were originally drawn mainly from two sources: 'An Interview with the Dalai Lama' by G.H. Mullin (AAP, New York, March 25 1976) and 'Der Dalai Lama' by Michael Hellbach (*200*, Germany, Summer 1978). These have been supplemented with a number of more recent interviews: 'I may be the last Dalai Lama' (*Newsweek,* March 14 1983), 'On Social Action and Tsampa' (*East-West Journal*, February 1984), 'Compassion is all-important' (*Washington Times*, Sept. 21 1984) and 'Dalai Lama, Seeker of Worldwide Peace' (*Logos, Tampa Tribune*, Oct. 13 1984).

This revised anthology marks a continuing attempt to set forth a wide spectrum of His Holiness' thoughts and activities, in that it attempts to show how he speaks to the Tibetan people, how he relates to the non-Buddhist community, Western and otherwise, his advice to international Buddhists, his views concerning his own political responsibility and his attitudes to the modern world. This has been done not through speculation or journalistic analysis, but purely through presenting speeches and articles by, as well as discussions with His Holiness himself. The reader is left to draw his or her own impressions and interpretations. We have not provided historical background to the articles, nor have we footnoted them, for we consider the pieces to be complete in themselves. The materials used here were chosen as being representative of His Holiness' views on the specific subjects involved and as embodying the sentiment of his presence.

Gyatso Tsering
Director (LTWA)
1984

CHAPTER I

The Buddhist Approach
to Knowledge

*(A discourse given to theTibetan Refugee Community,
New Delhi, 1963)*

The Buddhist Approach to Knowledge

Previously in Tibet on religious occasions all the people would go to the shrines and temples to make devotions. Poor and rich alike, businessmen and farmers, learned monks and illiterate nomads: all would come together to engage in spiritual practices.

Now a different fate has ripened for the Tibetan people. Due to our own bad karma, our country has fallen under the domination of a ruthless foreign invader. Our mountainous land of peace and calm has become a place of terror and great suffering. In place of the colourful dress that we Tibetans so much loved, the people are forced to wear alien uniforms signifying their position under an imposed Chinese communist scheme—officers, prisoners, labourers, exemplary volunteers, party members, reactionaries, and so on—and to live in a state of tension and fear. Their days and nights must pass in terror and insecurity. Few are the families who have not lost one or more members to the brutal Chinese oppression, or who do not have close relatives being held somewhere in the concentration camps. We here in voluntary exile may have difficulties as refugees, but at least we are free. We are not forced to attend indoctrination meetings every evening, nor told where we can and cannot go and what we can and cannot think, read or say. And what is most dear to every Tibetan heart, we are free to practise our religion.

There are many different religions in this world. Each of them has its own special qualities, its own unique way of presenting the spiritual path. We Tibetans chose Buddhism as our national religion. Buddhism is an especially satisfying and profound religion because it is not a path of faith but a path of reason and knowledge. Buddha himself stated that his doctrine should be accepted not on faith but only in the light of reason and logical inquiry. He also stated that many of his teachings were not literally true but required an interpretative approach, and therefore that his followers must personally weigh every point of doctrine to see if it is directly valid or only figuratively so. He advised that any teachings which do not fit practical situations and do not hold up under the weight of logical investigation should not be accepted. Because he taught over a period of many years to many types and levels of beings—to peoples of great, middle and small intelligence—his teachings require careful analysis.

3

Great Indian masters such as Nagarjuna and Asanga, both of whom were prophesied by Buddha himself, wrote many treatises on what teachings are literally true and what are merely figurative or for people of inferior understanding. Were all teachings literally true, there would have been no need for Buddha himself to have advised us to check up each teaching personally and to reject or reinterpret those which do not withstand logical investigation. Nor would there have been a need for him to have prophesied the coming of Nagarjuna and Asanga to elucidate his doctrines. Therefore Buddha did not ask us to accept everything that he taught; he advised that we personally check and recheck each teaching and practise only those which meet our own standards of logic and reason. In this way we are enabled to put into practice those teachings which are in harmony with our own level of development and capacity, and to see the other teachings in an according light. The different schools of Buddhism have largely arisen due to this facet of the teachings, with each school stressing a specific aspect of the doctrines as being fundamental and literal, and placing teachings other than this as peripheral and figurative. Thus Buddha presented an approach to his doctrine that is both vast and profound.

Had Buddha not relied upon truth in his teachings, were his teachings mere superstition, he would not have advised us to critically judge his words in this way. Instead, he would have given us a dogma like, "Believe what I say or else you will come to experience misery." The fact that he always advocated reason over blind acceptance indicates that his doctrine is founded on truth not fiction. The more we analyse a superstition or a falsity, the weaker becomes our belief in it, whereas the more we investigate truth, the stronger our belief becomes. This is the nature of truth and falsity. In my last meeting with Mao Tse Tung, he told me, "Religion is poison. It harms mankind and gives no benefit. It has poisoned Tibet and Mongolia." When he said this, I could not believe him; and the more I thought it over, the stronger became my disbelief in his words. On the one hand he had not looked deeply enough into the general purpose and effects of religion, and in particular was ignorant of the profound philosophical teachings of Buddhism. Therefore he thought that Buddhism was not relevant to present-day reality. He witnessed certain cases in which religion was used by some monks to extract an easy living from simple-minded people and concluded that all religion is merely a method whereby clever people seek to escape work and to live in ease. Mao was not an evil

4

or a bad man; he just misunderstood many things in life, religion being an important one of them.

As I said earlier, every religion has its own qualities and its own approach. The mark of Buddhism is that it is essentially humanistic rather than formally religious in its presentation. It attempts to define the problems confronting our lives and to set forth a number of remedies to these problems. Unlike most world religions, it does not hinge on the concept of God. It speaks of man and of how he can gain perfection. Many religions begin with the idea of a God and then use this idea to resolve all the problems confronting existence, such as creation and evolution. Although this is an easy answer, it is not logically provable. Therefore Buddha avoided it and tried to present a doctrine that in every way could be established through reason.

By avoiding the use of the God-theory, Buddha also avoided the many problematic side-effects that come with it. For example, one danger of centering one's doctrine on the concept of God is that the people can come to feel themselves overly humbled: they can worship God and perhaps one day even get to sit at His feet, but they can never equal Him. God is one entity and we humans, beings merely His creations, are destined forever to be inferior to Him. We can blindly accept and practise what He says or we can suffer the consequences of defying our Creator and Sustainer. This has the positive effect of lessening one's ego and the teachings to be practised, such as morality, love, devotion, etc., are always useful. But there is the danger that people will not appreciate the full greatness of the human potential. Also, religions based on the God-theory usually do not permit rejection of the 'Words of God', even should they contradict all reason. This can very easily stunt the growth of philosophical inquiry. Furthermore there are a number of philosophical problems immediately created by the presentation of the God-theory, such as, for example, if God is all-powerful and if He created everything and is now sustaining it, then He also created all the suffering and injustice. Thus we can conclude that He is extremely cruel and evil, like a mother who purposely gives birth to a child just to torture it and to submit it to great pain. In order to avoid these kinds of problems, Buddha tried to present a doctrine based purely on reason, and a path expressed solely in terms of human problems and human goals. He declared man himself to be responsible for his present existence, and provided a number of methods whereby this present state in which we find ourselves can be evolved and cultivated until perfection itself is attained. He pointed to man himself as being the

5

maker of his own destiny, the agent responsible for his own evolution or degeneration. The Buddhas are not Creators; they are but teachers and guides for those who would listen. Whether or not a person chooses to take advantage of their guidance is up to the individual himself or herself.

According to Buddhist scriptures, the creator of the world as we now know is nothing other than the ripening force of our own previous deeds or karma. Every action we ever create establishes an imprint on the mind that contributes to our future evolution. In brief, happiness is always a product of creative activity and suffering of negative activity. Moreover, negative activity and actions arise solely as a result of a deluded mind and positive actions as a result of a positive mind. Therefore, the aim of all religious practice is to cultivate and strengthen positive, creative states of mind and to eliminate negative, destructive states. A mind thus cultivated is both disciplined and calm and gives peace to the person who possesses it as well as to all with whom it comes in contact. We can easily witness its immediate effects upon both the individual and the society, and we can also clearly see the negative effects of a destructive mind. The far-reaching effects, which extend over years and lifetimes, are of course more subtle and require highly developed perception or logical reasoning to fathom. In the case of the Chinese invasion of Tibet we can see the immediate effects of the uncivilised and inconsiderate act of aggression in the number of the dead left on both sides and in the ill-feeling left in the wake of the invasion. It will of course breed only hatred and more violence. From the Chinese side, the cause is the presence of delusions such as greed and lust for power; and from the Tibetan side, the cause is the previously collected negative karma which in turn was created by delusion. If one's mind is spiritually evolved, one no longer creates this type of problem for oneself or others. For this reason Buddha said: "A spiritually evolved mind itself is happiness; a deluded mind is suffering." Because of this attitude, Buddhism lays its greatest emphasis not upon belief in anything or anyone but upon the practical cultivation of a positive, wholesome, creative mind, and upon the elimination of emotional afflictions such as greed, anger, attachment, ignorance so forth. This automatically leads to the increase of happiness and to the decrease of misery for both oneself and others.

Buddha once said, "You are your own saviour or you are your own enemy." This applies to all of us. Take myself, for example. If I try to cultivate goodness and the positive mind within myself, I am my own saviour. On the other hand, if I permit negativity to overpower my stream of being, I become my own destroyer. Had Mao seen religion in this light, I do not think that he could have called it poison.

These days many Asian scholars are talking about the similarities between Buddhist and communist social views. It is true that they have a lot in common, but there are a number of fundamental differences. For instance, communism places its emphasis upon materialism, upon the things of this life whereas, although Buddhism recognises the importance of a stable material basis, it is essentially a spiritual view and sees the material world as a tool with which to develop more lasting, inner qualities. In other words, the communist is primarily concerned with the body, which is lost at death, whereas the Buddhist is concerned primarily with the mind, which goes on into future existences. In terms of the two levels of truth—the deeper reality and the conventional, relative truth—communism concentrates upon a superficial level of the latter while Buddhism feels that in order for the latter to be really understood the former must be clearly known. In brief, communism thinks mainly about how people can fill their bellies, while Buddhism, although recognising the importance of a full stomach, sees the mind as ultimately being at the basis of both happiness and sorrow and therefore, more like the modern psychologist, seeks to create a state of mental harmony within people and thus to enable them to cope with all life situations more effectively. It tries to generate a condition of spiritual enlightenment within them by exposing them to deeper levels of reality.

As I said earlier, Buddhism is a path of reason and logical inquiry. In Tibet, however, perhaps because we were born with it as our religion, we often took it for granted. Many people therefore embraced its practice not on a basis of profound understanding but purely out of faith as an unconscious development in their lives. Thus their practice was like a castle built on ice, and when they were forced out of their natural environment by the Chinese invasion, it degenerated and collapsed. For those with a firm basis, however, the change reinforced and deepened their faith. Their contact with different values and views, such as Western science and technology, deepened their understanding of and conviction in Buddhist practice. Thus the Chinese taught us an important lesson, and we should be grateful to them for it. We should learn from it, and in future should rely upon an understanding based upon our own reasoning rather than upon quotations from Buddha, Long Chenpa or Tsong Khapa. Almost everyone in Tibet was Buddhist and therefore our beliefs were rarely challenged, whereas this is no longer the situation. We should

7

follow the approach of the Indian master Dharmakirti, who questioned everything and thus gained an unshakeable understanding of every teaching. In his *Pramanavartika* he examines subjects like karma, past and future lives, the relationship between mind and body, the concept of a beginning and an end to cyclic existence, the possibility of liberation and Buddhahood, and so forth, in a very critical way. We should develop our understanding of these topics along the lines he indicated, and perhaps write a few commentries updating his ideas.

The dividing line between a Buddhist and a non-Buddhist is that the former is someone who takes refuge in the Three Jewels: the Buddha—who is the teacher and the goal to be attained; the Dharma—the teachings and the path to be realised; and the Sangha—the holders of the robes and the advanced practitioners of the Dharma. Again, it is very important that this refuge is taken on the basis of a deep understanding of what these Three Jewels signify. Merely to call oneself a Buddhist is of little value; one must have the inner experience of dissatisfaction with mundane existence and the recognition that refuge in the Three Jewels, together with the spiritual practice that this refuge implies, will help one transcend this mundane state of being. Then one should gain a firm understanding of the karmic laws of cause and effect and exert oneself at developing harmony with them. In brief, we should make every effort to purify our mindstreams of negative traits and to develop every positive quality, such as love, compassion, detachment, higher meditation, wisdom and so forth. We must take direct responsibility for our own spiritual lives and rely upon nobody and nothing, for even the Buddhas of the 10 directions and three times are unable to help us if we do not help ourselves. If another being were able to save us, surely he or she would already have done so. It is time, therefore, that we help ourselves. At the moment we are blessed with human life and with all the possibilities that this implies. Unlike animals and lower life-forms, we are able to pluck the fruit of enlightenment, an act of ultimate goodness to both ourselves and others. However, death is pressing upon us from every side, threatening to rob us of this precious opportunity at any moment, and when we die nothing can be taken with us but the seeds of our life's work and our spiritual knowledge. A king loses his kingdom, and a crippled beggar leaves behind even his walking stick. We should quickly seize enlightenment while we still have the chance. In much less than a century all of us here will be dead. Maybe someone will say, "The Dalai Lama once gave a sermon here." Only this faint memory of today will remain. We cannot be sure that we will be alive even tomorrow. There is no time to procrastinate. I who am giving this teaching have no guarantee that I will live out this day. I hope that my life will be as long and fruitful as that of Gedun Drub, the First Dalai Lama (1391-1474), for at the moment many people are depending upon me; but who knows? Therefore I practise as intensely as I can, and advise you to do the same. But do not practise blindly, practise with a basis of wisdom and understanding. Then your spiritual strength will grow more vast and profound each day, and no matter what circumstances life throws upon you, your progress along the path will be undaunted. Our life here as refugees in India is not easy, but if we rely upon the practice of Buddhadharma it can be an excellent catalyst for spiritual development. And hopefully within a few years or decades we will be able to return to our country and to the loved ones we were forced to leave behind. Let's pray for this end, and make every effort that it may be realised.

Here I have just expressed a few thoughts that came into my mind. There is no seal on the mouth of the Dalai Lama, the Buddhist monk Lobsang Tenzin Gyatso. If there is anything you like in what I said, fine. If not, no problem; all you have to do is reject it. Do not accept anything merely because it was said by someone called 'the Dalai Lama'. Accept it only if it seems reasonable to you and of benefit to you and your spiritual life.

CHAPTER II

Universal Responsibility
and
The Good Heart

Edited materials from the informal talks and discussions given by His Holiness the XIV Dalai Lama on His first visit to the West, 1973

Part One: Informal Talks

When I first landed in the West, I noticed a number of rather superficial things which seem to differentiate the West from the East, and particularly from my own country, Tibet. It was, however, easy enough to understand these superficial differences in terms of the different cultural, historical and geographical backgrounds which have shaped a particular way of life and behaviour pattern. But in my mind I always feel that you are a human being, just as I am one, and that we are all basically the same: we are all human beings. The differences are really minor; the essential thing is that we are all human beings and in that respect we are all the same. I want happiness but not suffering, just as you do. And just as I have a right to obtain happiness, you also have an equal right.

Therefore, there is no fundamental difference between the East and the West or between you and me. Such differences as seem to exist are superficial and superimposed in many ways which cannot and should not separate man from man. Whenever I meet 'foreigners', I feel there is no barrier between us; to me such meetings are man-to-man relationships, heart-to-heart contacts.

The need for a man-to-man relationship is becoming increasingly urgent. Today the world is becoming smaller and smaller, more and more interdependent. We all depend very much on each other. In ancient times problems were mostly family-sized and were therefore tackled at family level, but now the situation is no longer the same. Today we have become so interdependent and so closely connected with each other that without a sense of universal responsibility our very existence and survival would be difficult. For example, one nation's problems can no longer be solved by itself entirely or satisfactorily, because much depends on the attitude and co-operation of other nations. Therefore I believe that for human happiness, human action based on concern for others is necessary. Throughout the ages a number of teachers belonging to different faiths have tried to teach the same kind of ideas and I think that today we need it perhaps more than ever before.

Unless we have a sense of universal responsibility, the same feeling for other people's suffering that we feel for our own suffering, in other words a good heart, it is difficult to achieve human happiness and world peace. I feel a natural heart-to-heart human relationship, transcending all artificial barriers like colour and creed, can solve many of the problems that plague us today. In this way we can know each other's way of thinking and achieve a better understanding, a real understanding, unfettered by inhuman considerations.

If we are able to develop a better understanding among ourselves, then on the basis of that understanding we can share and try to overcome the suffering of others and achieve happiness for others. I feel the few should be willing to sacrifice for the many. Let us compare ourselves, you and I: you are clearly in the majority while I am a single individual. Therefore I consider you (the audience) are much more important than myself, because you are in the majority.

Compassion for others (as opposed to self) is one of the central teachings of Mahayana Buddhism. In this connection I would like to quote a verse which conveys the message:

> If you are unable to exchange your happiness
> For the suffering of other beings.
> You have no hope of attaining Buddhahood,
> Nor even of happiness in this present life.

This means that if you are able to do the opposite of what the verse says, you will not only be able to achieve the ultimate goal, Buddhahood, but you will also be able to overcome your everyday problems and attain peace of mind through this practice. The essence of the Mahayana School, which we try to practise, is compassion. In Mahayana Buddhism you sacrifice yourself in order to attain salvation for the sake of other beings.

Avalokitesvara is conceived of as the 'Lord of Mercy' but the real Avalokitesvara is compassion itself. In other words, Avalokitesvara symbolises an ideal quality most valued by the Tibetans. It is this quality which we must strive to cultivate in ourselves from a limited quantum to the limitless. This undiscriminating, unmotivated and unlimited compassion for all is obviously not the usual love that you have for your friends, relatives or family. The love which is limited to your near and dear ones is alloyed with ignorance, with attachment. The kind of love we advocate is the love you can have even for someone who has done harm to you. This kind of love is to be extended to all living beings and it *can* be extended to all living beings.

The development of a kind heart, or feeling of closeness for all human beings, does not involve any kind of the religiosity we normally associate with it. It is not just for people who believe in religion; it is for everyone, irrespective of race, religion or of any political affiliation. It is for anybody who considers himself first and foremost a member of the human family and who sees things in larger terms. In any case, are we not brought up in love by our parents right from the time of our birth? Do we not agree that love plays an important part in human life? It consoles when one is helpless and distressed, and it consoles when one is old and lonely. It is a dynamic force that we should develop and use, but often tend to neglect, particularly in our prime years when we experience a false sense of security. The rationale for loving others is the recognition of the simple fact that every living being has the same right to and the same desire for happiness and not suffering, and the consideration that you as one individual are one life-unit as compared with the multitude of others in their ceaseless quest for happiness.

Viewed thus, individual happiness ceases to be a conscious self-seeking effort; it automatically becomes a by-product, but by no means inferior in quality or quantity, of the whole process of loving and serving others. According to the Mahayana School of Buddhism you must not only think in terms of human beings in this regard but of sentient beings. And ultimately all sentient beings have the potentiality to attain Buddhahood.

Therefore, taking into account the three points we have been discussing, namely, the desire, the right and the possibility of achieving happiness and avoiding suffering, and always keeping in mind one's relative unimportance in relation to others, we can conclude that it is worthwhile to sacrifice one's own benefit for the benefit of others. When you are trained in this kind of outlook, a true sense of compassion, a true sense of love and respect for others becomes possible and in due course a reality.

An enlightened outlook is not moralistic or religious in the conventional sense; it is not only good for those to whom such an approach is compassionately applied, but is beneficial to the individual himself as well. Our everyday experience confirms that a self-centred approach to problems can be destructive not only to society but to the individual himself. It does not solve problems, it multiplies them. For instance, when we encounter some problems, if we point our finger at ourself and not at others this gives control over ourself and calmness in a situation where otherwise self-control becomes problematic. If, on the other hand, when something bad happens we point at others and blame them, then our anger, hatred or jealousy, all these bad thoughts increase, and as a result we no longer feel happy. For example, when we are agitated we will not even have proper sleep, so we will ultimately suffer. For others also, when we develop or increase bad thoughts and feelings, our neighbours and friends will also feel disturbed. Instead, we should do just the opposite; put the blame on ourself for all the bad things, respect others and love others. If we do this it leaves others as well as ourself at peace. This is the essence of Mahayana Buddhism.

I shall illustrate what I have been trying to say by quoting some verses. The first verse says:

> I consider all living beings
> More precious than 'wish-fulfilling gems'—
> A motivation to achieve the greatest goal:
> So may I at all times care for them all.

The second verse is also extremely beneficial in our daily life:

> May I consider anyone I come to associate with
> Always more virtuous than myself.

Therefore, even if someone harms or hurts us badly, we should think of his good qualities and thus develop humility towards others.

The most important verse is the one which follows:

> If one whom I've helped my best
> And from whom I've expected much
> Harms me in a way I can't imagine:
> May I regard such a person as my best teacher!

This person is our greatest teacher for, when we are in a good mood and when our close friends are not criticising us, there is nothing to make us feel aware of the bad qualities we have. But when a person criticises us and exposes our faults, only then are we able to discover our faults and make amends. So our enemy is our greatest friend because he is the person who gives us the test we need for our inner strength, our tolerance and our respect for others. He is therefore a true teacher from this point of view. Instead of feeling angry with or hatred towards such a person, we should respect him and be grateful to him.

Although I have drawn examples from the Mahayana School of Buddhism, the aim of developing true friendship, brotherhood, love and respect for others is something which in essence is found in all religions. Religions contribute towards achieving peace of mind and serenity, but it

16

is not necessary for a person to be a follower of a particular religion in order to achieve it. He could employ Buddhist techniques of achieving peace of mind by cultivating certain qualities without becoming a Buddhist. It seems to me that these inner qualities are really human qualities. If we have these—compassion, love and respect for others, honesty and humility—then we can call ourself a real human being. Anger, attachment, hatred, jealousy and pride, all these bad qualities are our common enemies. If we want to be really good human beings we must cultivate the good qualities and then we will have less trouble, fewer problems.

Today we face a number of problems. Some are natural calamities, which we must accept and face as best we can. But some others are man-made problems created by our own misbehaviour, bad thoughts, which can be avoided. One such problem arises from ideological or even religious conflicts when men fight each other for means or methods, losing sight of human ends or goals. All different faiths and different systems are only methods to achieve a goal which for the average person is happiness in this life. Therefore at no time should we place means above ends: the supremacy of man over matter and all that it entails must be maintained at all times. The different ideologies, systems and religions of the world are meant for mankind to achieve human happiness.

I have learnt a great deal from other people during my tour. Tibet was materially backward in the sense that Tibetans in the past never enjoyed the comfort and luxury you have as a result of scientific discoveries and technological advancement. But, spiritually, Tibet was very rich. Apart from Buddhism which took deep root in the country, many great ancient sciences, arts and ideas from her neighbouring countries found their way into Tibet, which gradually became a melting pot of great Asian civilisations. Before this tour, we took Tibet's spiritual greatness for granted and almost ignored our material backwardness.

What amazed me during my tour is that many of you in the West seem to be very much worried about the material progress that you have made. I have heard a great deal of complaint against the material progress that has been made and yet paradoxically it has been the very pride of the Western world. I see nothing wrong with material progress provided man takes precedence over progress. In fact it has been my firm belief that in order to solve human problems in all their dimensions we must be able to combine and harmonise external material progress with inner mental development.

In my opinion material progress is certainly highly necessary and is a good thing, as it is of benefit to mankind. What is essential and would be more beneficial is that we should be able to balance material progress with mental development. By the various talks that I have had during the last few days with people from different walks of life, I am convinced that man must be placed above materialism, and that we must realise the true value of human beings. Materialism should serve man and not man serve material progress. And as long as we keep our goals and methods in their proper perspective, material progress will continue to benefit mankind.

I have liked science and technology since my childhood and I realise now more than ever before that material progress is highly necessary to mankind but at the same time I believe material things provide us mainly with physical comfort, not with mental peace. As I have already mentioned, good human qualities—honesty, sincerity, a good heart—cannot be bought with money, nor can they be produced by machines, but only by the mind itself. We can call this the inner light or God's blessing or human quality. This is the essence of mankind.

To this human end different religions have a very important role to play. Despite different conceptions of the universe, life after death, etc., all religions are essentially the same in their goal of developing a good human heart so that we may become better human beings. Of course, if you are out to find differences among religions, you will find plenty. This is only obvious. But the essence of religion is the development of a good heart, a true sense of brotherhood, love and respect for others.

Those of you who have taken an interest in Buddhism or have even become Buddhists, have done so because you have found it suitable to you. It is not good to change one's religion for the sake of it or because of one's dislike for some other religion. Religion is at best a tool to help us to train our mind in some desirable direction. Religion exists in order that we may practise something that will help us to control our mind; the aim is to transform the bad self-destructive thoughts—like anger, avarice, pride, jealousy, hatred—into their direct opposites. On recognising the destructive nature of bad thoughts, we practise religion in order to overcome them and in Mahayana Buddhism we do so not for ourself only but for the sake of all other beings.

In religion there are no national or man-made boundaries. Religion can and should be used by any people or person who find it beneficial. What is important for each seeker is to choose the religion which is most suitable to himself. However, I believe that the embracing of a particular religion like Buddhism does not mean the rejection of another religion or one's own community. In fact it is important that those of you who have embraced Buddhism should not cut yourselves off from your own society; you should continue to live within your own community and with its members. This is not only for your sake but for others' also, because by rejecting your community you obviously cannot benefit others, which actually is the basic aim of religion.

In Tibet there used to be a few Tibetan Christians. They followed the Christian faith but remained very much Tibetan. There is a verse by an ancient Tibetan teacher which says that you must change your mind but your external behaviour should remain as it is. We should also respect other religions. As I said earlier, the essence of all religions is basically the same: to achieve a true sense of brotherhood, a good heart, respect for others. If we can develop these qualities from within our heart, then I think we can actually achieve true peace.

Above all, we must put others before us and keep others in our mind constantly: the self must be placed last. All our doings and thinking must be motivated by compassion for others. The way to acquire this kind of outlook is that we must accept the simple fact that whatever we desire is also desired by others. Every being wants happiness, not suffering. If we adopt a self-centred approach to life by which we attempt to use others for our own self-interest, we might be able to gain temporary benefit but in the long run we will not succeed in achieving even our personal happiness, and hope for the next life is out of the question.

Part Two: Questions and Answers

1. AIM OF THE VISIT

Q: What do you aim at in your present travels around the world?

A: To be able to meet various people, to meet thinkers of the West.

Q: What may come out of those meetings, do you hope?

A: I have certain ideas which I want to exchange with those people. Today we have many problems: certain problems are mainly due to our own attitude and how we look at things, and because of this I feel that if we can change the mental attitude or outlook towards these things, much can be accomplished. In this respect it is extremely important to take into consideration right now how we are going to educate the younger generation. The present overall world situation itself is in such a condition that despite the fact that many know what is right and what is wrong, very often they are compelled by situations and circumstances to indulge in wrong actions. I had similar talks with His Holiness the Pope on these points.

2. IMPRESSIONS OF THE WEST

Q: Your Holiness, you have been in several European countries in the last few weeks. Have you detected any one or more common factors and features about the life in those countries?

A: Most of them are very similar. In this respect my attitude towards other people is that I always feel they are human beings. From this viewpoint, wherever I go, wherever I am, I feel just the same. Now I come from the East, particularly Tibet which has been isolated for many years, but in the deeper sense there is no difference. On the surface there are many differences, but these are minor. I always feel this, therefore among the European countries I have found fewer differences.

Q: What is the impression of Your Holiness during your first trip, of the people in the Western world, of the ordinary man?

A: The impression I have is to a large extent also influenced by my own attitude towards others. As I mentioned earlier, I always look at everyone as a human being, I don't put emphasis on the differences but emphasise the similarity, as a human being. For example we are meeting here; I am looking at you as a human being, not as an extraordinary human being, or a Westerner or German or anything like that, but just as a human being. So I always feel there is no barrier if I adopt such an attitude—this is a human being just like me. This is very helpful for me personally in easily accepting any situation. Of course the West is highly developed, has a high standard of living which is very important and for life it is necessary, so material progress is very good. Now the question is to balance or combine human values and material progress. If you concentrate everything on material progress, and lose all the human values, then that would be dangerous, that is not correct. Material progress itself is meant for human beings. Now if you have lost human values then it is of course wrong, but I feel there are many people who are interested in a combination of material progress and inner development.

Q: Your Holiness, may we ask you to tell us about your impressions on your trip to Europe until now?

A: The high standard of living which is very good and very important. But at the same time other problems are also being created because of this material progress. People complain about the noise, pollution, overcrowding, less mental peace—these kinds of things. Our very life itself is a paradox, contradictory in many senses; whenever we have too much of one thing then we have problems created by that. We always have extremes and therefore it is very important to try and find the middle way, to balance the two.

Q: May I raise the old Kipling question: can East and West meet? I am not thinking in a political sense, but in a spiritual one.

A: I feel that it is possible and in fact it is necessary also, because there is a need to create a universal responsibility; this is very important. Whether Easterner or Westerner, everybody is basically a human being: superficial differences are there, but deep down we are all the same, we have the same feelings. Whatever is good and comfortable every one of us wants, whatever is uncomfortable, like suffering, we try to avoid and every one of us has the same right to this. On the basis of such a thinking it is possible to build the whole world into one family, a family which doesn't have internal friction. That is the only solution, the only answer.

3. Main Human Problems

Q: Would you like to say a little more about what seem to you to be the main human problems at the moment? What do you see as the part of the human problem with which we should be most concerned? Is it attachment to material things in the West, is it our lack of any religious sense?

A: We are all human beings, we are all the same; everybody wants a happy life and does not want suffering and everybody has the right to try and achieve happiness and avoid suffering. But in some parts of the world there are quite high living-standards and facilities and in other parts there is poverty, hunger and disease and these sorts of things. Now if we accept that these are all the same human beings with the same equal rights, it is a sad thing, the situation is quite unfortunate. Secondly, today in the society of human beings everybody is talking about peace and justice but when we are facing certain problems it is difficult to put these qualities into practice because of the overall circumstances or overall pressure. But if in the society of human beings there is no justice, no truth, if everything is done through money or power, then it would be extremely unfortunate, very sad.

4. Materialism

Q: Materialism is a philosophy which sees material things as all-important. How can we help people who do not believe in spiritual things to develop spiritual values?

A: The best is to set a good example yourself.

Q: You believe that both material and mental progress are good and can exist side by side. How does Your Holiness think the two of them, often contradictory, can develop at the same time and in harmony— the mental and the material progress?

A: This is my aim; in fact, the object of my visit to Europe is also mainly based on this. It is quite obvious that without material progress we will lack many comforts, so we must have material progress. In the meantime, without inner peace material things alone are not sufficient. There are many signs which indicate that material progress alone is not sufficient for man, that there is something lacking. Therefore the only way is to combine these two. As to how they should be combined, here again I think it is very complicated and many factors will have to be taken into consideration. I firmly believe that if we take a liberal outlook, a broad outlook, and if we plan properly, this combination can be possible, not only by a few individuals or a few nations, but worldwide. Of course it is very difficult.

5. UNIVERSAL RESPONSIBILITY

Q: You have particularly spoken about the universal feeling that should be created among men. How does Your Holiness feel that this universal feeling can be achieved and in what way can religion, for example Buddhism, contribute to this universal feeling?

A: I am fully convinced that there is a great need for this development of universal responsibility. I also feel there are many ways and methods of trying to develop this kind of a feeling and as yet I am still trying to find which method would be the most suitable. My impressions are: I feel that one way is by developing a liberal outlook and also having a wider perspective; like for example when you are faced with a problem, not looking at it from a close distance but looking at it from a wider perspective. If you are able to do this then you are able to have better foresight. I feel that today we try to solve many problems temporarily, we don't investigate the real cause of the problems; for example it is like treating a sore by just trying to cure it without investigating what the basic cause of the sore is.

Another way, which I basically think is the most important, is this feeling for others, a feeling of closeness, trying to share the sufferings of others. In my opinion these are the two ways of achieving this universal responsibility. But the most important responsibility lies with the younger generation; an educational system where there is bad influence should be avoided as far as possible. For example when you see too much violence on television or other parts of the mass media, I feel that it has a great influence on the person.

Q: But how can the individual develop this feeling of universal responsibility?

A: We have to emphasise the importance of this and also try and put it into practice. Even today we have individuals as well as organisations who stress the importance of these points and I feel these need more emphasis; it is necessary to expand the influence of these organisations. But it is very difficult and it also takes time. That is why I place more hope on future generations rather than on the present. The present generation is living in this world under great pressure, under a very

23

complicated system, amidst confusion. Everybody talks and speaks about peace, justice, equality, but in practice it is very difficult. This is not because the individual person is bad, but because the overall environment, the pressures, the circumstances are so strong, so influential. I feel that perhaps the younger generation have a very heavy responsibility to achieve something.

Q: Where does religion enter this context? Is it possible to develop this feeling of universal responsibility without religion?

A: Yes.

Q: Would you say that religion should be the servant of man rather than man the servant of religion?

A: Yes. Religion does help to develop the right attitude of mind, it is important.

Q: What basic values should this universal responsibility be based on? What is right and what is wrong?

A: I feel the basis is that every one of us does not want suffering and every one of us wants something comfortable or happy in life. There is a verse which says that just as your physical body would not like the slightest pain, so you have to realise that the other being also has a similar feeling. For example, when you talk about rights, like human rights, the question is what do these rights fundamentally boil down to. Fundamentally they boil down to the feeling of 'I' and on the basis of that feeling we want happiness and bliss and we do not want suffering. And just as we have these desires, our fellow-being has similar desires; therefore what we have a right to, it is not correct to say that others do not have a right to. On the basis of these rights that we have and the rights that others have, if we believe these are similar, then others have rights also. Now if we compare which is the more important, each one of us is just one single person whereas the others are limitless. There are thousands of millions of people, therefore, the others are much more important, because each of us is just one individual. I feel that this way of thinking is a democratic way of religion.

Q: Would His Holiness please tell us how it is practical to observe and practise this love of humanity in a world such as ours today?

A: This is the really difficult point, yet we have no alternative but to make an attempt towards this. In order to do so I think there are many ways, many methods of doing this. It is my hope that some special study or research on this point could be carried out in order to make a thorough investigation of this important matter. I am not saying this in connection with religion but in connection with human happiness. To put it in other words, it is a question of the survival of mankind and it would be difficult to explain in detail how it should be done because it would be very lengthy.

6. RELIGION

Q: Does Your Holiness think that the very special kind of Buddhism practised in Tibet in its original form could benefit European people?

A: Yes, for some people it would be of benefit, because for religion there is no national boundary. Even among Tibetans we have Christians as well as Muslims. We are all the same. What is important is the faith or religion which is more suitable to you.

Q: Does the Dalai Lama think that the values of Buddhism in Tibet will spread or be useful in the Western countries?

A: Perhaps there are some things that can be picked out from it. In any case religion is something for all men, it is a common property, there are no man-made boundaries for that. It should be used for any people or for any person for whom it may be found beneficial. I believe that each religion has its own qualities, its own values. Also for these past many centuries the various different kinds of religion have benefitted, in their own way, the many different kinds of people on this earth.

Q: In your opinion what is the essence of religion?

A: Compassion.

Q: Would His Holiness like to say more about this purpose of religion, as he understands it?

A: I feel that the purpose of religion is basically in order to attain peace and happiness for mankind. Christians say love for God, love for neighbour, love for fellow being. This is my personal interpretation of Christianity. And just as you have love for God, love for your neighbours, so the purpose of having love for God is to be able to make yourself close to God. If you are close to God you have a motive to listen to His voice, and His voice or teaching is that we should love one another. Basically the most important thing is this love for others. In Buddhism also every emphasis is on love for others.

25

Q: We started with responsibility and spirituality; now we are on to love God and love your brother. What we are looking for is the moment when spirituality and responsibility become the same thing and when the love of God and the brother become the same experience. Can you help us to see how that is so?

A: Among all those who accept religion, each follower has his own sort of system, his own method in order to achieve that goal. I want to stress that it is not necessary for everyone to follow one path, nor is there only one way. Without faith, without belief, I am quite sure we can achieve this.

Q: Without faith?

A: Yes.

Q: Each person holds certain beliefs which he thinks are true and these are different from the beliefs held by other people, they are disagreeing. Can they all be right?

A: We cannot say that there is only one religion and that one religion is the best, or that a particular religion is the best. Now for example I am a Buddhist but I cannot say Buddhism is the best, although for me Buddhism is best. Generally we cannot say Buddhism is best. For certain people Christianity is much more influential than Buddhism, so for them Christianity is best.

Q: Can you tell us something about the influence of modernisation in Western countries on your religion?

A: I feel that there should be no contradiction. I think the essence of Buddhism is kindness, compassion. This is the essence of every religion, but particularly in Mahayana Buddhism. I think this is very important and everybody can practise it without deeper faith. Simply you are a human being; everybody appreciates kindness. In fact when we grow up, we grow up with the kindness of our parents and without that sort of kindness we cannot exist. This is very clear because today you find that children who are not brought up with the love of their parents, or where there is a disruption in the family, are later on psychologically affected. As a human being kindness, a warm heart, is very important. I always feel this is a very precious thing because you cannot buy this kindness or warm heart with money. In Europe there are very good shops but there's no shop which sells kindness; you must build it within. You can transplant hearts but you cannot transplant a warm heart. Maybe in the future some scientists might be able to transplant certain cells of the heart, which are kindness or something like that, which would be excellent.

7. The Good Heart

Q: Could you give a description of the character of the good person, the good man which we should all be like?

A: I think it is generally a good heart, kindness. If you have this basic quality of kindness or good heart, then all other things such as education, ability, will go in the right direction. If you have a bad heart, then knowledge or ability are used in the wrong direction; instead of helping others it makes trouble.

Q:* You spoke of the importance of the good heart. Do you think that all men have inherently the potential for a good heart, or that some may not possess it?

A: Every man has the basis of good. Not only human beings, you can find it among animals or insects, for instance when we treat a dog or horse lovingly.

Q: We would all feel, I expect, that one of the roles of religion as such is to protect the good heart from being spoilt by that which will make it evil.

A: Yes, if you take religion the right way. If you use religion the wrong way, then there is a holy war, or something like this may happen in the name of religion in the wrong way.

Q: Why then does everyone not have a good heart now? What is it that makes people bad?

A: There are more opportunities to develop the bad qualities. If one were to accept rebirth, then there are many reasons in the past and previous lives. If we take today itself, the present situation, maybe to a large extent environment would also play an important part. If the feeling or attitude of most of our neighbours is just a competitive and selfish motive, or some such atmosphere, then we will always feel isolated and also that there is no one we can trust. This is very bad. Ultimately compassion and respect for others diminish, because we may be put in a position where we find that unless we defend ourself there is no alternative; then we naturally hold a selfish motive.

Q: Are there not some things so evil that we should hate them?

A: Our own bad thoughts. The real enemy is not outside but inside. Now here, you see, it is necessary to make a distinction between external enemies and internal ones. External enemies are not permanent; if we respect him the enemy will become our friend. But there is one enemy who is always an enemy, with whom we should never compromise, and that is the enemy inside our heart. We cannot change all these bad thoughts into our friends, but we have to confront and control them.

9. UNITY OF RELIGIONS

Q: Your Holiness wrote in your book *My Land and My People* about unity of religions. Practically speaking, how or by what means could this unity ever be achieved?

A: As I explained before, just as each religion has its own respective philosophy and there are similarities as well as differences among the various religions, so we must go according to what is suitable for each individual. Just as in the world we have many different kinds of food—for example on my present tour of the ten European countries I have had quite a variety—so we cannot tell all the people that they must take one particular kind of food. What is important is what is suitable for a particular person. For example in the different food habits of different people we don't have any disputes, because each one takes what is suitable for him. Similarly religion is a food for the mind and as we all have different tastes we must take that which is most suitable for us. The important thing is that we must have peace of mind. Just as in Buddhism we have love of all beings, love for others, similarly in Christianity there is love for God, love for our fellow beings. In these the emphasis is similar, so the important thing is these similarities. As I said earlier, if we look from a wider perspective, I feel there are no problems, we can go together. It is impossible to make one religion and it would even be unnecessary. In fact if this were to happen it would be a great loss, because each respective religion has its own qualities and values, all of which would be lost.

Q: Is there not a resemblance between the two religions (Christianity and Buddhism)?

A: Yes, I agree with you; this is very true. If we look at different religions as instruments to develop a good heart, love for others, respect for others, a true sense of brotherhood, in these respects all religions are the same, because basically in all religions the purpose is to make man a better human being. All these different complicated philosophies were not meant to make man more confused, they were meant to help man transform himself into a better human being. Therefore the most important thing is to look at the purpose of religion, the main aim, not at the secondary things that are involved, and if we go in the right direction of looking at the main aim, then all religions can go together.

What I am most interested in discussing is that all the major religions of the world can contribute towards the peace of mankind, can act for the benefit of mankind, and what I wanted to know or discuss was how these different religions can best be used so that this goal can be achieved. In this 20th century we must particularly use religion, but how to use it in the best way, the most effective way? We will have to leave aside the different philosophies because that is the business of each religion. It would be impossible to make one religion, one philosophy, it is foolish; in fact we would be destroying many of the good characteristics of each respective religion.

9. PEACE OF MIND

Q: Is there any connection between peace of mind and world peace?

A: Oh, certainly. Without proper mental peace it is difficult to achieve proper world peace; therefore there is a connection. Many of the problems that we have today are because of our hatred. As a human being we have good qualities as well as bad ones. Now anger, attachment, jealousy, hatred are the bad side; these are the real enemy. From a certain point of view our real enemy, the true trouble-maker, is inside. So these bad thoughts remain active and as long as we have these it is difficult to attain mental peace.

Q: What would the first steps be to teach the young and also others peace of mind, as I understand this is the essential concern of His Holiness?

A: My approach to this is not purely from the Buddhist point of view, nor even from the religious point of view. In fact in order to achieve this peace of mind it is not necessary that a person must be religious. There are many people among non-believers who sacrifice their own lives for the benefit of the masses or the majority which means less selfishness, more respect for others. It is extremely important to realise that what we feel, what we want is exactly what others also want and feel. You are asking about the first step but in this respect I am just beginning to search for certain viewpoints on the matter. It is difficult to implement because although this kind of thing is very simple to talk about, when we have to put it into practice it is extremely difficult.

10. PROBLEMS OF YOUTH

Q: In the Occident, in Europe, we have quite a problem of generation; the relations between young and old people are somewhat difficult, the veneration of old age is lost. Do you have similar problems nowadays in Tibet, with Tibetan young people?

A: Yes, it is natural that there are some problems, but generally speaking in the Asian countries the relationship between children and parents is very good. There is a generation gap, but because the family relationship is usually harmonious, they respect each other, particularly the children respect their parents and elders.

Q: Can I say something about the mental unrest among young people? A lot of my friends, and myself included, really feel this unrest and that we are searching for something. But what is so dangerous is that we don't know how to understand what we are really looking for, so we get caught up in creeds, in the various things that are going around, and these stop people from thinking about what it is they are really missing. I was wondering if you had any ideas about how to make people really able to understand what it is they are searching for? I think they don't know what it is.

A: It is difficult to say what in particular you should follow, because for each individual it would differ; it may require a different method which is suitable for that person. But generally—of course I am a Buddhist and so according to the Buddhist viewpoint—the main thing is realisation of human beings. A human being is not just a part of matter but more than that. We are something else, we feel emotions; although it is very bad, it is the basis of all bad thoughts. But in any case we have these qualities, this nature, so a human being is above matter. Now on this basis comes the realisation of respect for others' rights, for other people also have the same feelings; therefore realise this and respect their rights. In other words, love for God is very important, but for me love for others is much more important. In this respect all religions say the same thing: love for others, respect for others. Christ sacrificing himself for man is a good example. If you have this feeling towards others, I think you yourself will feel happy and your neighbours or your friends will also feel much more comfortable. And as for you, patience is also important. It is difficult to achieve this in one moment; sometimes it takes time, so have patience. But of course I don't know, this is just my own feeling.

Q: I have reached the borders of your country once, but found the same trouble with institutions being a problem that we find here in trying to get anywhere. I wonder what you think about the problem of institutions in a wide sense being the greatest barrier that people have to some extent in communicating and spreading this happiness that you talk about? Because we have it and I don't think anyone in the West would deny that this is a huge problem. Is it the same for you and is it something you consider has to be fought? Power structures, institutions for the sake of institutions? Young people at least see this as a very difficult problem, only they don't go the right way about dealing with it. They try and confront power instead of trying to understand what makes people do things. Young people are very anti-authoritarian. They don't like somebody who gets up and says, "I know," or, "You come to me for advice, I know." This arouses great resistance amongst young people and I just wonder what your feelings are on this problem of power and authority?

A: First of all we will have to consider whether the authority is just or not. If it is just, then it is right and helpful to comply with it. But if it is unjust and unreasonable then I feel you have the right to rebel against it. This is just a straight answer to your question. Of course you have to take into consideration many factors that might be involved in taking a particular action. If you are talking with reference to certain social systems, traditional systems, then I agree with you 100 per cent. I hate formality and these things. You make yourself a prisoner, you pretend to be something else, you try to hide your real feelings and then make yourself a different person. Now if we want to change these traditional systems or institutions made by man we have the right to do so. The systems were not created to bind people but in order to help. They were made in order to create some sense of discipline or authority.

Q: I think what I am trying to ask you is about the method. Do you object violently if things become intolerable and totalitarian in any sense of institution, or does one go on hoping and trying to go in the inside to change things? This sounds very general, but I think you understand what I mean.

A: Yes. Of course I just mentioned these things. It is very difficult to generalise, but basically I am a firm believer in non-violence. Now here violence is a method, not the aim or goal, and it depends on the motive and the result. If the motive is good, not selfish but for the good of the mass or a large number of people, that sort of compassion, then the result is benefit for many. Here comes the method. In such circumstances if there is no other method but violence, then of course this is right—the motive is good, the result is good, there is no other means but violence, then it is good.

Q: My question is a very simple one. For many young people, certainly in the West, life can seem difficult. Old authorities cease to exist. In this kind of world, which from your own experience of life we know has been very varied and we know also the intense spiritual preoccupation, what advice would you give to a young person whether he is Jewish, Christian, Tibetan, Hindu? What would be your advice to them how best to live and make their contribution to a better and happier world?

A: This is difficult. I really don't know, but my suggestion or advice is very simple, that is: to have a sincere heart. I believe that this is something basic and that anyone can approach through this way, irrespective of whatever ideology he may belong to or even if he is an unbeliever. Real, true brotherhood, a good heart towards one's fellow men, this is the basic thing. I believe that if you have a true feeling of brotherhood then whether you are a scientist, an economist or a politician, whatever profession you may follow, you will always have this concern for your fellow beings. I also believe that if you have this concern for others, then whatever the effects that might result from the profession you follow, you will always be concerned as to whether it is going to benefit or harm your fellow beings. I personally feel that this concern for others is lacking today. Many people emphasise thinking only of oneself and having a selfish motive. I feel that basically the cause of many problems is due to this lack of concern for others and that if we really develop this kind of a sincere feeling and a sense of universal responsibility, then many of the problems we face today, like pollution, the energy crisis and the population crisis, can be solved. If we have such a sincere feeling we need not worry about the self-sufficiency of the world. What I am referring to is that today in certain parts of the world we have poverty and starvation and in other parts of the world abundance of wealth. This is an example. So if we have a genuine concern for others, then I feel that there is no need to suffer from such problems, because the world has sufficient resources to overcome these problems. The main thing is whether we have the real sense of universal responsibility. Basically then the most important thing is a good heart.

11. Drugs

Q: In the Occident, in Europe, we have an increasing problem with drugs, especially with young people. I would like to know whether drugs have ever been used, or still are used, in meditative practice in Vajrayana and are drugs at all a suitable means to deepen or broaden our consciousness?

A: Drugs are not used. Although I do not personally have any experience, from talking to people who have taken drugs I have the impression that by taking drugs you lose your discriminative power, the power to penetrate, and I feel that this would not be helpful for higher meditation.

Q: What do you think about drugs? Can they be beneficial or are they harmful?

A: Generally speaking drugs are not good. Mental development should be carried out by internal means, not through external means.

Q: People who take drugs claim they have enlightenment in the time it takes to snap your fingers. On what level or rather in what layer or sheath of the personality does this so-called enlightenment take place? Please explain also the danger of drugs.

A: I have no experience. Some people say it helps very much, but in any case my view is this: enlightenment or improvement or internal progress should be through mental practice, mental training, not by external means like drugs or injections or operations.

12. The Future

Q: Can you give us any picture of how you see the future, what it means to you?

A: It seems to me that this present atmosphere in the world is not very happy. Generally we know what is right and what is wrong, yet despite this knowledge we almost always take the opposite action; because of the pressure, of the atmosphere, we cannot act in the right way. So from my viewpoint at least this is certainly not beneficial, but we can change this. Therefore I have much more hope in the future, the younger generation. As I mentioned before the goal or aim is happiness for everyone. All mankind desires a happy life. In order to achieve that goal different people adopt different methods. Some people try to achieve it through science and technology, some through religious practices and some through different government systems, different ideologies. If we look at the main goal, then all the others are different methods to reach that goal.

Q: And you see the goal as happiness?

A: Yes. There are various kinds of happiness. Certain happiness like bliss is something much more deep, but the deeper or higher happiness or inner bliss cannot be achieved by the masses. A few individuals can achieve this, mainly through the Christian belief in God, and then as a Buddhist there are certain methods to achieve this higher bliss or happiness. But I am talking of general happiness, real peace and worldly progress. In this respect I always feel it is very important to develop universal responsibility, irrespective of different ideologies or faiths. Now the world is becoming smaller and smaller, we are dependent on each other. In such an atmosphere we must have universal responsibility. If we have this feeling, then I am quite sure we can solve many problems the right way, through peaceful means. This is my main topic for discussion. I realise it is rather difficult to make a good human being, but despite that it is worthwhile to try. It may take 50, 80, or 100 years, but as I am a religious person I feel it is reasonable to think this way and to try. In this field I want to know other people's views, especially in Western countries: the views of people who are born here, live here—this is my main reason for this visit.

Q: You look to the future but do you see in the present aspects of life that make you optimistic for the future and if so in which case, which particular things give you optimism?

A: I believe that this solution—the combination of inner development and material progress—is actually connected with the very survival of man himself. And you see, a good heart towards our neighbour, our fellow men, is something very important for life. If in the society of mankind there is really no justice, no truth, if everything is done by money and power, then it is rather difficult to live. Sometimes this atmosphere does have great influence. There are many good systems, for example democracy, and in each system there are many good

34

points. Of course there are bad points also, mostly caused by money and power. As human beings we must live on this earth not for our generation but for the next one, so if there is really no justice and no truth then it would be very sad and very unfortunate. This is my main concern. Also as an Easterner we have many problems like poverty and disease, lack of education. In the West you are highly developed in the material sense, the living standard is remarkably high, which is very important, very good. Yet despite these facilities you have mental unrest, for example among the youth and among politicians. This is not a healthy sign; it is a clear indication that there is something wrong, something lacking. So this is my theme and because of it I am a little optimistic.

Q: What do you see as the hope for the world working out its problems, from your Buddhist perspective? You say that love is the key but do you think that President Reagan and Mr. Chernenko can really love each other?

A: My thinking is not just for a few years, this president or that president. I am talking generations. I think in the next century a different shape will come. The present condition [is based on] a hostile attitude and making new weapons and spending millions of dollars, this side makes something new, and the other side sooner or later will get it. Many people, especially in Europe, remain in terror and fear. It cannot go on like this forever.

Another problem is the south and north problem, the rich and poor. And the ecology problem. There are many different kinds of problems. I believe the key point and future hope is our own mental attitude. We should be more open-minded and concerned about others' welfare.

Q: So you think things will get better by the next century?
A: I don't know. But I try my best, that gives me satisfaction. Success or not doesn't matter.

Q: Do you think the trigger for change will come from the religious world or the political world?
A: Both. Those and the scientists. Thinkers. Some scientists take a keen interest in harmony between nations.

13. NUCLEAR WAR

Q: Many people in the West are worried about nuclear war. What should people do about this?

A: First, you must see that it is worthwhile and important to make an individual effort to stop, or at least to minimise, the danger of nuclear war. To begin, of course, we must control the anger and hatred in ourselves. And as we learn to remain in peace, then we can demonstrate in society in a way that makes a real statement for world peace. If we ourselves remain always angry and then sing about world peace, it has little meaning. So you see, first our individual self must learn peace. This we can practise. Then we can teach the rest of the world.

On a larger scale, those people who really know the danger of nuclear weapons and how much damage can be done, such as doctors and scientists who can explain clearly, should use their voices and speak up. They might approach it technically, or explain in their own way, so that others will understand the frightful potential of these weapons. Then, from the spiritual side, they could speak about the importance of preserving human life.

Q: Is there anything else that can help prevent nuclear war?

A: We must see each other as people and not as enemies. I feel one way would be to have the leaders of the nuclear powers begin to talk to each other. Warfare and hatred are always based on misunderstanding about human happiness and on mistrust between people. If the leaders could meet directly they could start to see each other as people, as human beings, and there would be a chance for some understanding and compassion to grow. Even if these talks were not so friendly at first, they would give an opportunity for this understanding to develop. And meanwhile, during them, there would be more time to find other ways to help the situation. At least I hope so.

14. SOCIAL ACTION

Q: Your Holiness, how do we combine a spiritual life with social and political action? So many people separate them.

A: I feel that the essence of all spiritual life is our emotion, our attitude towards others. Once we have pure and sincere motivation, all the rest follows. We can develop this right attitude towards others on the basis of kindness, love and respect, and on the clear realisation of the oneness of all human beings. This is important because others benefit by this motivation as much as anything we do. Then, with a pure heart, we can carry on any work—farming, mechanical engineering, working as a doctor, as a lawyer, as a teacher—and our profession becomes a real instrument to help the human community.

Q: The Tibetan culture is so rich. What do you think is the most important thing that the West has to learn from Tibet and the teachings in the East?

A: Making tsampa [barley flour]! Tsampa and the pot of tea! Usually in our place we are making tsampa. The people who are working on it have powder of tsampa all the way from their tall hats to their feet—they get full of white.

More seriously, the Tibetan culture is rich mainly due to Buddha's teaching, I think. Central to Buddha's teaching is seeing the equality among humanity and the importance of the equality of all sentient beings. Whether we are Buddhist or not, this is something important to know and to understand.

Then we must also see the potential for developing a loving kind of patience, a tolerance founded on the basis of courage, not on the basis of pessimism. Tolerance and patience with courage are not signs of failure, but signs of victory. In our daily life, as we learn more patience, more tolerance with wisdom and courage, we will see it is the true source of success. Actually, if we are too impatient, that's a real failure.

All different religions carry the essence of these ideas or teachings, but I feel the Buddhist practices are especially profound and detailed, so maybe they can contribute to the West and even to Christianity. You can remain as a Christian, meantime taking some Buddhist technique.

Q: What can we do to help end the suffering in the world? What can one individual do?

A: We must each lead a way of life with self-awareness and compassion, to do as much as we can. Then, whatever happens, we will have no regrets.

All want happiness and not suffering. Even from insects on up, each being wants happiness. We are only one, whereas others are infinite in number. Thus, it can be clearly decided that others gaining happiness is more important than just ourself alone. From beginningless time up until now, we have brought ourselves into great difficulties through selfishness. We should turn this around and consider others to be more important. Beings such as animals of all kinds have no chance to understand this fact, whereas we are humans who have gained this fine human life where such can be understood. We have some intelligence and with that can understand the value of cherishing others and the faults of cherishing ourselves. We now need to implement this, to put it into actual practice, not just to leave it as understanding. We should think, "If I don't achieve this now, when could I possibly achieve it?"

Part Three: Kindness—A Simple Religion for Mankind

QUEST FOR HUMAN KINDNESS

My general belief is something quite simple. All sentient beings, particularly human beings, no matter whether they are educated or uneducated, rich or poor, Easterners or Westerners, believers or non-believers, each one wants happiness and does not want suffering. This is the nature of all sentient beings.

I believe happiness comes from kindness. Happiness cannot come from hatred or anger. Nobody can say, "Today I am happy because this morning I was very angry." On the contrary, people feel uneasy and sad and say, "Today I am not very happy because I lost my temper this morning." So you see this fact is something natural. Through kindness, whether at our own level or at the national or international level, through mutual understanding and through mutual respect we will get peace, we will get happiness and we will get genuine satisfaction. It is very difficult to achieve peace and harmony through competition and hatred, so the practice of kindness is very, very important and very, very valuable in human society. Here we don't need a deeper philosophy, we don't need monasteries, we don't need temples, we don't need images and so on, we don't need gods—we can simply practise kindness. Simply try to become a good human being; by a good human being I mean a warm-hearted person. To think of other people—complete selflessness is impossible but to be unselfish and more concerned about other people—that is the real Dharma or Religion, it is something very useful.

If we are kind people, we ourselves will feel deep satisfaction every moment and every day and other people, our immediate neighbours or even our enemies, will appreciate kindness. Through hatred and anger we will lose our own peace. When we become very angry, at that moment we lose a real human quality, that is the ability to judge, to think, what is right and what is wrong? If we almost go crazy with anger, then we can't judge the situation and an enemy might take advantage. On the other hand, if someone is doing something unreasonable, it may be necessary to take strong action to stop his unreasonable behaviour; even then we can manage without anger, it might be better not to lose patience or lose our temper. We should handle and tackle problems with a very normal mind capable of judging the situation.

In our daily life kindness is something very precious. I believe that kindness is the most precious thing and that as human beings we need kindness, particularly in this period of fear and anxiety. Here in Gangtok you may not feel anxiety, but if you go down to Calcutta, Bombay and Madras, you will feel some mental unrest or some kind of problem. Then if you go farther west to Europe or America, despite their beautiful material progress human problems are still there, if not more so, particularly due to the world power blocs, politically the East and West blocs and economically the North and South. All these problems are, I believe, man-made. If there is an earthquake or landslide we cannot help it, it is out of our hands, but these problems due to ideology and systems are man-made. So if we approach them in the right way we can minimise these problems even if we can't eliminate them completely.

Likewise in international politics I believe that human kindness is an essential point. Now in order to develop kindness the clear realisation of oneness of all kinds is important. If we make too many differences, too many barriers, too many boundaries then they will create more problems whether political or religious. Wherever I go, I go with this feeling that I am a human being, nothing special or strange. Physically I come from Tibet and when I was in America or the Soviet Union there appeared to be a big difference, but if we look deeper we see that the people of the U.S.A. are also human beings, they want happiness and do not want suffering and they equally have the right to be happy. Similarly, the people of the Soviet Union, people of this country, people of Tibet and the people of China— all are human beings and of the same human category. With this feeling I myself have found it much easier and simpler to make person-to-person contact, I don't feel any barriers. Now, today, we are here together, people from the plains, from other places and from Tibet, the Dalai Lama of Tibet, but basically we are all the same. Even our faces are basically the same with one mouth and two eyes, nothing special; my mouth is like this but nobody's mouth is like this (gestures and laughs)—with this sort of feeling I myself find more peace. Although many of you are meeting me for the first time, we have no particular barriers between us and this feeling helps us to respect each other.

Now, the difference comes when you see you are a lone person, you are one being while others are infinite. Now, which is more important, the benefit of the majority or the benefit of a single man? Nobody can say that a single person's benefit is more important than that of the majority, particularly these days when democratic ideas concern the benefit of the majority. Under these circumstances you and others both have the same desire and the same rights. You are single and other people are many, so it is absolutely worthwhile to consider other people's benefit first; you must come after them, then alone real kindness, real compassion and real love will grow. That kind of love and kindness is not because of a feeling that this is my wife, my children, my family and my parents, but because this is a human being, this is one kind of sentient being who needs happiness, who has a right to be as happy as I am. Other beings are the majority and are much more important than myself; with these feelings, kindness is based on deep reason and logic.

Our usual feeling of love and kindness is generally based on attachment, which in turn is based on ignorance. This is not sound and correct love; true kindness and true love must be based on logic and clear consciousness. So I believe that the practice of kindness is a universal religion, whether you are a believer, or even an anti-religionist like Chairman Mao Tse Tung. Theoretically he was anti-religion but in his work and advice one thing that struck me very much was that he mentioned the benefit of working people, that is, the majority of needy people and that in order to achieve the benefit of working people it is absolutely worthwhile to sacrifice one's own life. That is the essential point of religion or Dharma. Unfortunately there is a big gap between what we say and what we practise; but I feel this is essential, so I express it.

HARMONY BETWEEN DIFFERENT RELIGIONS

Basically all major religions of the world carry the same message, therefore harmony between different religions is both important and necessary. Fortunately, here in Sikkim, it seems you have good relations and harmony between different faiths which is very good and must be continued. Nothing can be achieved through sectarian feeling; for example, I am a Buddhist Bhikshu, but I firmly believe that all religions have the same potential to help mankind although they have big differences in philosophy. The other day I had a talk with the Governor of Sikkim about the fact that Buddhists do not believe in a Creator-God, and that similarly amongst Hindus one branch of Samkhya philosophers does not accept the theory of God, nor do Jains. In most other religions the central point of philosophy is God the Creator. Now if you look at that alone there is a big difference between religions, one believes in God and the other does not. But we should not look at that side or on that level only, we must investigate and discover the purpose of the theory of no-God. I think it is the same (as the God theory), it is to make a better human being. Human minds are so varied and different that one philosophy cannot suit all human beings, therefore many philosophies are needed to suit the many kinds of mentality.

Now, a good example is Mother Teresa, a good mother and a believer in God. She is such a kind person, having devoted all her energy to the needs of poor people, she is quite remarkable. This is the result of her practice of Christianity, yet in a Buddhist context her work would be the practice of a Bodhisattva. I cannot even compare myself to her and I don't know whether I could do what she does or not, so the difference in philosophy doesn't matter much. We must look into it until we see the purpose, then we will be able to respect and value her religion.

Usually I put it like this: different philosophies are like different dishes. If you always eat the same kind of food for breakfast, lunch and dinner then you will get fed up and won't want to eat any more, so it's better to have variety. Religion is similar, it's useful to have varieties of religion. Do you agree? I am glad. So, you see, harmony between different religions is very, very important.

CHAPTER III

From A Tibetan Buddhist Perspective

Brief essays on the theories, attitudes and practices of the Buddhist tradition as preserved in Tibet (translated from Tibetan sources by various devotees)

Part One: Traditions of Tibetan Buddhism

From very ancient times, Tibet and India maintained very close intercourse in the fields of culture, education, religion, literature and art. Thoughts and ideas of profound significance emanating from India and flowing freely into the fertile and receptive soil of Tibet brought about cultural and social changes of revolutionary magnitude. India was regarded not only as the fountain-head of many great philosophical ideas and systems but also as the source of spiritual inspiration and of initiatives leading to fruitful action. However, of all these influences, Buddhism stands out as the paramount cause of the splendid metamorphosis that changed the entire course of Tibet's history. The glorious light of wisdom, embodied in the noble doctrine of Buddhism, having spread throughout the countries of India, found its way into Tibet, and in the course of time became a sovereign power of unexcelled brilliance. Historically, the culture of Tibet is firmly rooted in the Buddhadharma. Generations of Tibetan intellectuals studied and developed a profound culture that closely accorded with the original principles and philosophy of the Dharma. Down through the centuries their dedicated services brought about extraordinary developments which are unique among the literary and cultural achievements of the nations of the world. A galaxy of Indian scholars gave Tibet their perennial wisdom and opened the eyes of Tibetans to vastly expanded horizons. This helped to form the Tibetan mentality, which delights in penetrating analysis and examination and in exploring the virgin fields of the mind, thus opening up boundless vistas of intellectual development. As a result, Tibetan thought was greatly enriched and this is one of the primary reasons why Tibetans have always regarded India with a peculiarly fervent veneration as the guide who led their country into wisdom's realm.

Prior to the introduction of Buddhism, Bon, a native tradition, was the dominant faith of Tibet. Recorded history tells us that Tibet received its initial impact of Buddhism when the first Indian pandit, Buddharakshita visited Tibet during the reign of Latho-thori, the 25th King of Tibet (who was later recognised as one of the earthly manifestations of the Samanatabhadra Bodhisattva). The way of Buddhism became pronounced in the seventh century A.D. when Thonmi Sambhota, a brilliant intellectual court minister, was sent to India by King Song-tsen-Gampo of Tibet for educational studies.

After studying for a number of years at the feet of numerous Indian pandits in the various branches of learning, Thonmi Sambhota returned to Tibet. He not only invented the letters of the Tibetan alphabet, the first of its kind in Tibet, but also translated the Karandavusutra (mDo-sde-za-ma tog) and Sachhipurnamudra (dPan-skong-phyag-rgya-pa) into Tibetan. Besides, Thonmi Sambhota in collaboration with various Indian scholars is reputed to have translated 21 Sutras from Sanskrit into Tibetan. These were the first Buddhist Sutras in Sanskrit to be translated into Tibetan. Thereafter, an extensive corpus of literature grew up. A host of Indian and Tibetan pandits and Lotsawas (scholar translators) set about translating into Tibetan the Sutras and Tantras brought from India and Nepal. The Kangyur, consisting of over 100 bulky volumes and the Tengyur, consisting of over 200 volumes, were both translated in full during this period.

The Lord Buddha bestowed upon the world his unique teachings which are enshrined in the systems commonly known as Hinayana and Mahayana, of which the latter includes the body of teaching known as Tantrayana. The Hinayana doctrine was handed down through a lineage of seven hierarchs, and its progress through the avenues of time was unimpeded and unrestrained. Unlike Hinayana, Mahayana did not progress smoothly, but suffered persecution at the hands of heretical and pagan forces on three different occasions. It was, therefore, considerably weakened.

Guru Padma Sambhava, a famous Tantric teacher from India (who is believed to have hailed from Dhanakosha Island), visited Tibet in the eighth century A.D. and preached the esoteric Vajrayana Doctrine (the Adamantine Wheel of the Great Mystery) to a group of 25 followers including King Tritsong De-Tsen. In the course of time, he founded the Nyingma School of Vajrayana in Tibet. In the 11th century A.D., Dipankara Srijnana, an outstanding scholar from Vikramshila University in India, came to Tibet and taught Sutras and Tantras extensively. His disciples such as Khonton, Ngok and Drom founded the Kadampa School in Tibet.

Towards the end of the 11th century A.D. Marton Chokyi Lodroe, a famous Tibetan translator, paid three visits to India, during which he studied at the feet of such stalwarts as Pandit Naropa, and after returning to Tibet, undertook an extensive translation and propagation of the knowledge gained from those far-famed Indian scholars. Later on, the doctrine which he propounded and handed down through Jetsun Milarepa and Nyam-may Dagpa Lharje came to be known as Kagyud.

In the 12th century A.D. Khon Konchok Gyalpo inherited the doctrine of Lam-Dres (the Path and the Enlightenment) from Drokme Lotsawa. This doctrine was preserved and fostered through five hierarchs of Sakya Lamas, and their followers came to be known as the Sakya sect.

In the 14th century A.D. there emerged a famous figure called Jamgon Je Tsong Khapa, who is reputed to have made a thorough study of the inner meaning of the entire corpus of Sutras and Tantras. The lineage established by his followers such as Gyaltshab Je and Khedrub Je is known as the Gandenpa or Gelug Sect.

Besides these, there are a number of subsidiary sects founded by learned individuals in Tibet.

Admittedly, there are a few differences between Mahayana and Hinayana in their way of expressing the teachings; but the ultimate goal of both schools is identical in that both aim at helping sentient beings to attain the supreme status of Buddhahood. The entire esoteric system (Vajrayana) of the Doctrine has been classified into two distinct groups—internal and external, between which there is a great difference. The people of Tibet regard the Sutras and Tantras which they preach and practise as being firmly rooted in the Lord Buddha's teachings. Whenever further elucidations are required, they consult works containing the excellent conclusions arrived at by the learned Indian scholars of whom I have spoken. Then commentaries of Nagarjuna, Aryadeva, Buddhapalita, Chandrakirti, Shantideva and so on are held in special esteem, and are frequently referred to. Indeed, it is traditionally held that the teachings and commentaries expounded by those learned Indian scholars are the sole source to which one can turn for clarification of the Sacred Doctrine.

In conclusion, I wish to observe that the sages and pandits of India and Tibet have bequeathed to us the wisdom and experience they acquired by long years of diligent study, practice, meditation and reflection. Their noble efforts contributed to building up a bridge which has united the people of our two countries like children of the same family. This unique relationship will remain forever as a perfect example of international fraternity and understanding.

Part Two: Happiness, Karma and the Mind

Many billions of years elapsed between the origin of this world and the first appearance of living beings upon its surface. Thereafter it took an immense time for living creatures to become mature in thought—in the development and perfection of their intellectual faculties; and even from the time men attained maturity up to the present, many thousands of years have passed. Through all these vast periods of time, the world has undergone constant changes, for it is in a continual state of flux. Even now, many comparatively recent occurrences which appeared for a little while to remain static are seen to have been undergoing changes from moment to moment. One may wonder what it is that remains immutable when every sort of material and mental phenomenon seems to be invariably subject to the process of change, of mutability. All of them are forever arising, developing and passing away. In the vortex of all these changes, it is Truth alone which remains constant and unalterable—in other words, the truth of righteousness (Dharma) and its accompanying beneficial results, and the truth of evil action and its accompanying harmful results. A good cause produces a good result, a bad cause a bad result. Good or bad, beneficial or harmful, every result necessarily has a cause. This principle alone is abiding, immutable and constant. It was so before man entered the world, in the early period of his existence, and in the present age; and it will be so in all ages to come.

All of us desire happiness and the avoidance of suffering and of everything else that is unpleasant. Pleasure and pain arise from a cause, as we all know. Whether certain consequences are due to a single cause or to a group of causes is determined by the nature of those consequences. In some cases, even if the cause factors are neither powerful nor numerous, it is still possible for the effect factors to occur. Whatever the quality of the result factors, whether they are good or bad, their magnitude and intensity directly correspond to the quantity and strength of the cause factors. Therefore, for success in avoiding unwished for pains and in acquiring desired pleasures, which is in itself no small matter, the relinquishment of a great number of collective cause factors is required.

In analysing the nature and state of happiness, it will be apparent that it has two aspects. One is immediate joy (temporary); the other is deeper joy (ultimate). Temporary pleasures comprise the comforts and enjoyments which people crave, such as good dwellings, lovely furniture, delicious food, good company, pleasant conversation, and so on. In other words, temporary pleasures are what man enjoys in this life. The question as to whether the enjoyment of these pleasures and satisfactions derives purely from external factors needs to be examined in the light of clear logic. If external factors were alone responsible for giving rise to such pleasures a person would be happy when these were present and, conversely, unhappy in their absence. However, this is not so. For, even in the absence of external conditions leading to pleasure a man can still be happy and at peace. This demonstrates that external factors are not alone responsible for stimulating man's happiness. Were it true that external factors were solely responsible for, or that they wholly conditioned the arising of, pleasure and happiness, a person possessing an abundance of these factors would have illimitable joy, which is by no means always so. It is true that these external factors do make a partial contribution to the creation of pleasure in a man's lifetime. However, to state that the external factors are all that is needed and therefore the exclusive cause of happiness in a man's span of life is an absurd and illogical proposition. It is by no means sure that the presence of such external factors will beget joy. On the contrary, factual happenings such as the experiencing of inner fortitude and happiness despite the total absence of such pleasure-causing external factors, and the frequent absence of joy despite their presence, clearly show the cause of happiness to depend upon a different set of conditioning factors.

If one were to be misled by the argument that the above-mentioned conditioning factors constitute the sole cause of happiness, to the preclusion of any other conditioning causes, that would imply that (resulting) happiness is inseparably bound to external causal factors, its presence or absence being exclusively determined by them. The fact that this is obviously not so is sufficient proof that external causal factors are not necessarily nor wholly responsible for the effect phenomenon of happiness.

Now what is that other internal set of causes? How are they to be explained? As Buddhists, we all believe in the law of karma, the natural law of cause and effect. Whatever external causal conditions someone comes across in subsequent lives result from the accumulation of that individual's actions in previous lives. When the karmic force of past deeds reaches maturity, a person experiences pleasurable and unpleasurable mental states. They are but a natural consequence of his own previous actions. The most important thing to understand is that, when suitable (karmic) conditions resulting from the totality of past actions are there, one's external factors are bound to be favourable. The coming into contact of conditions due to (karmic) action and external causal factors will produce a pleasurable mental state. If the requisite causal conditions for experiencing interior joy are lacking, there will be no opportunity for the occurrence of suitable external conditioning factors; or, even if these external conditioning factors are present, it will not be possible for the person to experience the joy that would otherwise be his. This shows that inner causal conditions are essential in that these are what principally determine the experience of happiness (and its opposite). Therefore, in order to achieve the desired results, it is imperative for us to accumulate both the cause-creating external factors and the cause-creating internal (karmic) conditioning factors at the same time.

To state the matter in simple terms, for the accrual of good inner (karmic) conditioning factors, what are principally needed are such qualities as having few wants, contentment, humility, simplicity, other noble qualities. Practice of these inner causal conditions will even facilitate changes in the aforementioned external conditioning factors that will convert them into characteristics conducive to the arising of happiness. The absence of suitable inner causal conditions such as having few wants, contentment, patience, forgiveness and so on, will prevent one from enjoying pleasure, even if all the right external conditioning factors are present. Besides this, one must have to one's credit the force of merits and virtues accumulated in past lives. Otherwise, the seeds of happiness will not bear fruit.

The matter can be put in another way. The pleasures and frustrations, the happiness and suffering experienced by each individual are the inevitable fruits of beneficial and evil actions he has perpetrated, thus adding to his store. If, at a particular moment in this present life, the fruits of a person's good actions ripen, he will recognise, if he is a wise man, that they are the fruits of (past) meritorious deeds. This will gratify him and encourage him to achieve more merits. Similarly, when a person happens to experience pain and dissatisfaction, he will be able to bear them calmly if he maintains an unshakeable conviction that, whether he wishes it or not, he must suffer and bear the consequences of his own (past) deeds, notwithstanding the fact that normally he will often find the intensity and extent of his frustration hard to bear. Besides, the realisation that they are nothing but the fruits of unskilled action in the past will make him wise enough to desist from unskilled deeds henceforth. Likewise, the satisfying thought that, with the ripening of past (evil) karma, a certain part of the evil fruit accrued by former unskilled action has been worked off, will be a source of immense relief to him.

A proper appreciation of this wisdom will contribute to grasping the essentials for achieving peace of mind and body. For instance, suppose a person is suddenly afflicted with critical physical suffering due to certain external factors. If, by the force of sheer will-power (based on the conviction that he is himself responsible for his present misery and sufferings), he can neutralise the extent of his suffering, then his mind will be much comforted and at peace.

Now let me explain this at a rather higher level. This concerns the strivings and efforts that can be made for the systematic destruction of dissatisfaction and its causes.

As stated before, pleasure and pain, happiness and dissatisfaction are the effects of one's own good and bad, skilled and unskilled actions. Skilful and unskilful (karmic) actions are not external phenomena. They belong essentially to the realm of mind. Making strenuous efforts to build up every possible kind of skilful karma and to put every vestige of unskilful karma from us is the path to creating happiness and avoiding the creation of pain and suffering. For it is inevitable that a happy result follows a skilful cause; and that the consequence of building up unskilful causes is suffering.

Therefore, it is of the utmost importance that we strive by every possible means to increase the quality and quantity of skilful actions and to make a corresponding paring down of our unskilful actions.

How is this to be accomplished? Meritorious and unmeritorious causes which result in pleasure and pain do not resemble external objects. For instance, in the human bodily system, different parts such as lungs, heart, and other organs can be replaced with new ones. But this is not so in the case of karmic actions, which are purely of the mind. The earning of fresh merits and the eradicating of bad causes are purely mental processes. They cannot be achieved with outside help of any kind. The only way to accomplish them is by controlling and disciplining the hitherto untamed mind. For this, we require a fuller comprehension of the element called mind.

Through the gates of the five sense organs a being sees, hears, smells, tastes, and comes into contact with a host of external forms, objects and impressions. Let the form, sound, smell, taste, touch, and mental events which are the relations of the six senses be shut off. When this is done, the recollection of past events on which the mind tends to dwell will be completely discontinued and the flow of memory cut off. Similarly, plans for the future and contemplation of future action must not be allowed to arise. It is necessary to create a vacuum in place of all such processes of thought if one is to empty the mind of all such processes of thought. Freed from all these processes, there will remain a pure, clean, distinct and quiescent mind. Now let us examine what sort of characteristics constitute the mind when it has attained this stage. We surely do possess something called mind but how are we to recognise its existence? The real and essential mind is what is to be found when the entire load of gross obstructions and aberrations (i.e. sense impressions, memories, etc.) has been cleared away. Discerning this aspect of real mind, we shall discover that, unlike external objects, its true nature is devoid of form or colour; nor can we find any basis of truth for such false and deceptive notions as that the mind originated from this or that, or that it will move from here to there, or that it is located in such-and-such a place. When it comes into contact with no object, mind is like a vast, boundless void, or like a serene, limitless ocean. When it encounters an object, it at once has cognizance of it like a mirror instantly reflecting a person who stands in front of it. The true nature of mind consists not only in taking clear cognizance of the object but also in communicating a concrete experience of that object to the one experiencing it. Normally, our forms of sense cognition, such as eye-consciousness, ear-consciousness, etc., perform their function on external phenomena in a manner involving gross distortion. Knowledge from sense cognition, being based on gross external phenomena, is also of a gross nature. When this type of gross stimulation is shut out, and when concrete experiences and clear cognizance arise from within, mind assumes the characteristics of an infinite void similar to the infinitude of space. But this void is not to be taken as the true nature of mind. We have become so habituated to consciousness of the form and colour of gross objects that, when we make concentrated introspection into the nature of mind it is, as I have said, found to be a vast, limitless void free from any gross obscurity or other hindrances. Nevertheless, this does not mean that we have discerned the subtle true nature of the mind. What has been explained above concerns the state of mind in relation to the concrete experience and clear cognizance by the mind which are its function, but it describes only the relative nature of mind.

There are in addition several other aspects and states of mind. In other words, taking mind as the supreme basis, there are many attributes related to it. Just as an onion consists of layer upon layer that can be peeled away, so does every sort of object have a number of layers; and this is no less true of the nature of mind as explained here—it, too, has layer within layer, state within state.

All compounded things are subject to disintegration. Since experience and knowledge are impermanent and subject to disintegration, the mind of which they are functions (nature) is not something that remains constant and eternal. From moment to moment, it undergoes change and disintegration. This transience of mind is one aspect of its nature. However, its true nature, as we have observed, has many aspects, including consciousness of concrete experience and cognizance of objects. Now let us make a further examination in order to grasp the meaning of the subtle essence of such a mind. Mind came into existence because of its own cause. To deny that the origination of mind is dependent on a cause, or to say that it is a designation given as a means of recognizing the nature of mind aggregates, is not correct. To our superficial observance, mind, which has concrete experience and clear cognizance as its nature, appears to be a powerful, independent, subjective, complete, ruling entity. However, deeper analysis will reveal that this mind, possessing as it does the function of experience and cognizance, is not a self-created entity, but is dependent on other factors for its existence. Hence it depends on something other than itself. This non-independent quality of the mind substance is its true nature which, in turn, is the ultimate reality of the self.

Of these two aspects viz. the ultimate true nature of mind and a knowledge of that ultimate true nature, the former is the base, and the latter an attribute. Mind (self) is the basis, and all its different states are attributes. However, the basis and its attributes have from the first pertained to the same single essence. The non-self-created (depending on a cause other than itself) mind (basis) and its essence, shunyata, have unceasingly existed as the one, same, inseparable essence from beginningless beginning. The nature of shunyata pervades all elements. However, as we are now, since we cannot grasp or comprehend the indestructible, natural, ultimate reality (shunyata) of our own minds, we continue to commit errors and our defects persist.

Taking mind as the subject and mind's ultimate reality as its object one will arrive at a proper comprehension of the true essence of mind, i.e. its ultimate reality. And when, after prolonged, patient meditation one comes to perceive and grasp at the knowledge of mind's ultimate reality which is devoid of dual characteristics, one will gradually be able to exhaust the delusions and defects of the central and secondary minds such as wrath, love of ostentation, jealousy, envy, and so on.

Failure to identify the true nature of mind will be overcome through an acquisition of the power to comprehend its ultimate reality. This will, in turn, eradicate lust and hatred and all other secondary delusions emanating from the basic ones. Consequently, there will be no occasion for accumulating demeritorious karma. By this means the creation of (evil) karma affecting future lives will be eliminated; one will be able to increase the quality and quantity of meritorious causal conditioning and to eradicate the creation of harmful causal conditioning affecting future lives—apart from the bad karma accumulated earlier.

In the practice of gaining a perfect knowledge of the true nature of mind, strenuous and concentrated mental efforts are required for comprehending the object. In our normal condition as it is at present, when our mind comes into contact with something it is immediately drawn to it. This makes comprehension impossible. Therefore, in order to acquire great dynamic mental power, the very maximum exertion is the first imperative. For example, a big river flowing over a wide expanse of shallows will have very little force; but when it passes through a steep gorge, all the water is concentrated in a narrow space and therefore flows with great force. For a similar reason all the mental distractions which draw the mind away from the object of contemplation are to be avoided and the mind kept steadily fixed upon it. Unless this is done, the practice for gaining a proper understanding of the nature of mind will be a total failure.

To make the mind docile, it is essential for us to discipline and control it well. Speech and bodily activities which accompany mental processes must not be allowed to run on in an indiscreet, unbridled, random way. Just as a trainer disciplines and calms a wild and wilful steed by subjecting it to skilful and prolonged training, so must the wild, wandering, random activities of body and speech be tamed to make them docile, righteous, and skilful. Therefore the teachings of the Lord Buddha comprise three graded categories, that is, Shila (Training in Higher Conduct), Samadhi (Training in Higher Meditation) and Prajna (Training in Higher Wisdom), all of them for disciplining the mind.

Studying, meditating on and practising the three grades of Trisiksha in this way, one accomplishes progressive realisation. A person so trained will be endowed with the wonderful quality of being able to bear patiently the miseries and suffering which are the fruit of his past karma. He will regard his misfortunes as blessings in disguise, for they will enlighten him as to the meaning of nemesis (karma) and convince him of the need to concentrate on performing only meritorious deeds. If his past (evil) karma has not as yet borne fruit, it will still be possible for him to obliterate this unripe karma by utilising the strength of the four powers, namely: 1. Determination to attain the status of Buddhahood; 2. Determination to eschew demeritorious deeds even at the cost of his life; 3. The performance of meritorious deeds; and 4. Repentance.

Such is the way to attain immediate happiness, to pave the way for attaining liberation in future, and to help avoid the accumulation of further demerits.

Part Three: Combining the Three Vehicles

The methods employed for the practice of the Buddhadharma (the teaching of the Lord Buddha) are diverse, for they depend upon the capacity and inclination of the individual mind. This is because those to be trained are not endowed with a uniform standard of intelligence. Some people have a sharp intelligence while others are gifted only with mediocre understanding. Accordingly, the Lord Buddha delivered His teaching to suit varying degrees of intelligence and receptivity. Notwithstanding these many levels of instruction, it is still possible to provide a description of the general method of practising the Buddhadharma as a whole. From the doctrinal standpoint, the Buddhadharma can be said to consist of four schools, of thought. These are: (i) Vaibhasika, (ii)Sautrantika, (iii) Vijnavada and (iv) Shunyavada. In terms of practice, the Buddhadharma is classified into three categories, also known as the three vehicles, viz. (i) Sravakayana or Hinayana, (ii) Pratyekabuddhayana and (iii) Bodhisattvayana or Mahayana. As Sravakayana and Pratyekabuddhayana are basically of the same form, they are commonly known as Hinayana. So we have the two main vehicles—Mahayana and Hinayana. Mahayana is further subdivided into the vehicles of Prajnaparamitayana or the 'Cause Vehicle of Perfection' and the Vajrayana or the 'Effect Vehicle of the Adamantine Wheel' which is also known as the 'Great Secret'.

Whether one practises Mahayana or Hinayana, the 'Cause Vehicle' or the 'Effect Vehicle of Mahayana', each of these is a valid form of the glorious teaching of the Lord Buddha. Sometimes it may happen that a person who has not made a proper study of, or not yet fully realised, all these doctrines of the Blessed One will find himself puzzled by what appear to be some elementary contradictions between the concepts of Mahayana and Hinayana, or of Sutra and Tantra. For indeed the Buddhadharma does have different and contradictory aspects, namely permissive and prohibitive precepts, within the vast concourse of its philosophical system. This gives rise to different and varying forms of practice and conduct. Only by delving deeply into these seeming contradictions, after equipping oneself by a deep study and by clearly comprehending the body of Lord Buddha's teaching in all its aspects, will one acquire a comprehensive knowledge of the methods and systems of its procedure and practice.

When this knowledge has been attained, the realisation will dawn upon the seeker that those permissive and prohibitive aspects of the Buddha's teaching have both been designed to advance the practitioner gradually and progressively along the right path, according to his capabilities and his intellectual development. In other words, the aim of all the yanas is to discipline the defiled and untamed mind of the individual, and to strengthen and clarify the precepts in accordance with the progressive development of his mind.

Then in what way can the teaching be fully carried out by a person practising the Buddhadharma? A Tibetan saying answers the question in the following way.

> Outward conduct is practised in accordance with Vinaya (Hinayana).
> Inwardly, mental activity is practised with Bodhi-mind (Mahayana)
> Practised in secrecy is Tantra (Vajrayana).

The above may be exemplified as follows. A Shramanara or Bhikshu, having pledged himself to observe the vows, acts in accordance with the rules of the Vinaya. Such a person is then motivated with the thought of attaining the status of Buddhahood for the liberation of all sentient beings. He therefore strives to practise the 'six perfections' and the 'four attributes' of a Bodhisattva. (The six perfections are: generosity, morality, forbearance, perseverance, collectedness and wisdom. The four attributes are: charity according to the needs of the recipient, courtesy in speech, encouraging others to practise virtues, and guiding others in the practice of virtues.) Apart from this, he also trains himself in the two principal ways of meditation according to the esoteric teaching. In this manner, he will be practising all the teaching of Mahayana, Hinayana, Sutra and Tantra. This process is similar to that found in all the writings of the great Indian teachers.

"Outward conduct is practised in accordance with Vinaya." This can be explained as follows: there are eight categories of moral rules concerning the outward conduct practised in accordance with Vinaya discipline. The most important among them are the ones meant for Bhikshus. Bhikshus have to observe 253 rules of Vinaya. There are other secondary rules, but the set of 253 is the most important. They mostly concern the speech and physical conduct of Bhikshus.

The second saying, i.e. "Inwardly, mental activity is practised with

Bodhi-mind" means that the Bhikshu or the person concerned is motivated with the thought of liberating all sentient beings and also of acquiring the wisdom which perceives shunyata (Void). Equipped with such motives, he seeks to acquire the attributes of Sublime Thought as set down in the Transcendental Wisdom of the Mahayana and to achieve the great qualities emanating from the Sublime Thought.

The explanation of the third saying, "Practised in secrecy is Tantra" is that, in order to fulfil the great and glorious task of liberating all sentient beings, for which the status of Buddhahood is to be attained within the shortest time possible, the method of Tantra (Esoteric Teaching) is practised in secret. Tantra is unlike the other methods, being a distinct and special method, unique in character. It prepares and conditions the body in a special way for treading the path to that goal.

In this way, a person finally completes the progressive practices involved in all the methods—Mahayana, Hinayana, Sutra and Tantra. Just as a doctor prescribes different kinds of diet in accordance with the progress in a patient's health so does a person practise these different methods as his mind progressively develops during his journey towards enlightenment. The aim of all of them is to train the mind of the individual.

Tantra is classified into four divisions:

1. Kriya Tantra: this stresses the importance of purifying external activities.
2. Charya Tantra: this stresses the parallel importance of both external and internal (mental) activities.
3. Yoga Tantra: this stresses the importance of internal (mental) activities, i.e. meditation.
4. Anuttara Yoga Tantra: this stresses the supreme importance of inner activity, regardless of the purification of external activities, i.e. it involves a higher type of meditation.

No special methods have been enunciated in the Kriya Tantra, Charya Tantra and Yoga Tantra for the subtle meditative concentration on the various life centres of the physical body that regulate and control the breathing, the movement of seminal fluids and blood circulation, whereas methods for such purposes are found in abundance in Anuttara Yoga. Nonetheless, when anyone is practising any one of these four classes of Tantra, the first thing required of him is the preparation of his mind, technically known as the 'ripening of the mind'. For this he must receive the requisite formal initiation from a competent teacher into the secret form of spiritual knowledge. The next step is observance of the sacred vows and rules of conduct prescribed in the Tantric teachings. In the case of the first three classes of Tantra, the person proceeds to the practice of the mental activity of concentrating on the non-self-existing (shunyata) nature of the deity. In the case of the fourth one practises the path of the Utpanna Krama leading to maturity, and the path of the Sampanna Krama leading to freedom. At the stage of Utpanna Krama, the initiated person identifies himself with the person of the deity which he has taken as the object of meditation. Only when he has achieved the power of meditation in the Utpanna Krama can he proceed to the next stage of Sampanna Krama. In Sampanna Krama the person concentrates on acquiring the power of controlling the system of his breathing, blood circulation and the procreative forces of semen. Through these processes he advances to the acquirement of the status of Buddhahood. This, in other words, means that the person will acquire the power resulting from the self-existing body (Svabhavakaya), truth body (Dharmakaya), beatific body (Sambhogakaya), and emanation body (Nirmanakaya), and the five kinds of divine wisdom.

The methods which will aid in the practice of the Buddhadharma (as explained above) can be briefly summarised as follows: first and foremost, one has to gain a complete understanding of the meaning of the method to be practised. For this, one must listen to numerous sermons, lectures and explanations on the subject from adepts. The meaning of what they teach must be pondered again and again, whereafter comes the next step of performing a concentrative meditation on the meaning pondered. These three processes should be combined in equal proportions without neglecting any one of them. This will make one become the true possessor of three great qualities, namely learning, nobility and virtue. A learned man will become noble only when he puts into real practice what he has learnt, and not by mere words. Similarly, a noble man who has gained complete control over his mind but is lacking in extensive knowledge of discourses and precepts will fall short of the definition of being learned. He must become genuinely proficient in a wide variety of subjects that come under the purview of the Buddhadharma. The achievement of these two requirements plus the acquirement of the motive to do good for others will make a person truly come to possess the three qualities of being learned, noble and good.

Part Four: Between Misery and Joy

The faculty of reasoning distinguishes man from animals and other living creatures. Human beings are capable of investigating and understanding many things which animals cannot. Because they are able to discover and perceive things lying beyond the direct perceptions of their sense-organs, most men, whether they are Buddhists, Hindus, Christians, or belong to any other denomination offer up prayers or devotional recitations of one kind or another. Are such prayers and recitations due merely to custom, are they mere rituals to embellish daily life? The answer is definitely negative, because controlling and disciplining the mind is or should be the primary purpose of all prayers and religious recitations.

Though there are various methods of disciplining the mind, to think primarily for the benefit of others is immensely important. Benevolent thought for others will bring happiness both to them and to oneself, whereas if one thinks only of one's own selfish comfort and happiness, nothing but suffering can result. As the great Indian Pandit Shantideva has said: "All suffering in this world is due to egoistic desire for selfish comfort and happiness. All happiness is the fruit of selfless desire for the comfort and happiness of others."

Happiness, whether it is transient or ultimate, is a direct or indirect result of a sincere desire for the welfare of others. The main cause of suffering is egoistic desire for one's own comfort and happiness or its indirect effects. In this strife-torn world of ours, this is always true, no matter whether the sufferings in question are on a large scale such as those resulting from disagreement between different nations or the perpetration of a wicked act which brings about the loss of many lives, or on a smaller scale such as the bickering between insects. In all such cases, egoism is the root cause.

When mutual co-operation between neighbours and nations is motivated by benevolent thoughts for each other, such motivation is of the highest value. It is fitting that we should attach greater importance to unselfish desire for the comfort and happiness of others than to egoistic desire for self-beatitude and happiness. Generally speaking, all beings possessing mind feel discomforted when they come across something unpleasant which they cannot appreciate, however trivial it may be.

Knowing that others, too, suffer when they encounter things that discomfort them, one should make every effort to avoid doing anything that might be the cause of discomfort or suffering to another being. This principle can be the foundation of peace and of all means of bringing about or consolidating world peace, such as disarmament. When all thoughts likely to cause suffering, such as a desire to resort to violence, are erased from the mind then speech and action, which stem from thought, will be devoid of evil intent. Similarly, the success of disarmament and other peace movements stems from a determination to achieve peace which first takes form in the mind and is subsequently translated into speech and action. Speech and action unsupported by firm intention in the mind will achieve nothing, howsoever one may try. Basically, the inability to control and discipline the mind is at the bottom of all the troubles and problems of the world. Therefore, in this life of ours, whether we believe in rebirth or not, if we generate and send our benevolent thoughts towards all beings from men down to the tiniest insects, the world will inevitably be a happier place to live in. Happiness is gained for oneself and others by concentrating chiefly on others. What the world needs today is compassion and love. It is, therefore, of the utmost importance that we cultivate kindly thoughts for others so that thinking fondly of their welfare becomes an ingrained habit of mind.

Part Five: Sects and Sectarianism

What exactly do we mean when we use the word 'religion' as a term common to all our doctrinal systems? By referring to the Latin roots of the word, we can trace its origin to the prefix *re-*(again) and the verb *ligare* (to tie up); therefore the primitive meaning of 'religion' would seem to be 'to bind again'. Now how does the concept of binding up or tying up come to be applied as the common term for all our various teachings? The common enemy of all religious disciplines, the target of all moral precepts laid down by the great teachers of mankind, is selfishness of mind. For it is just this which causes ignorance, anger and passion which are at the root of all the troubles of the world. The great teachers wanted to lead their followers away from the path of negative deeds caused by ignorance and to introduce them to the path of righteousness. They all agreed that the prime necessity for this is to bind up and control the undisciplined mind which harbours selfishness; for, with their great wisdom, they saw it to be the origin of all ill. Therefore, we can find in the very word which embraces all our spiritual teachings the key to and foundation of unity and harmony. We can easily ascribe the superficial disparities of dogma and appellation to the differences of time, place, culture, language, etc., prevailing at the time each religion came into being. By concentrating on the actual practice of each individual devotee, we shall discover with absolute certainty that we share the same sublime aim. To cite the great mentor, the saint-scholar Tsong Khapa:

> All precepts when realised are found free of contradiction.
> Every teaching is a precept for actual practice.
> This is the easy way to penetrate to our Teacher's meaning,
> And to avoid the great ill of abandoning the path.

The spirit of non-contradiction expressed in this so-called 'Path of the Quadrangle' provides the key to a broad philosophical acceptance of the spirit and function of religion. For by maintaining sharp awareness of the function as expressed in the actuality of all teachings, we can escape the ruinous error of sectarian discrimination and partisanship, and we can avoid the grave sin of casting aside any religious teaching. It gives me great pleasure to repeat these words which were spoken long ago in the

Land of Snows; for I am sure they will make an outstanding contribution to the development of unity and of a spirit of co-operation which are vital to keeping alive the flame of the spirit and preserving discipline in these difficult times of strife and partisanship all over the world.

To make use of an analogy: a skilled physician ministers to his patients individually, giving each the appropriate medicine necessary to cure his particular disease. Furthermore, the method and materials of treatment will vary according to the particular combination of circumstances of time and country. Yet all the widely differing medicines and medical methods are similar in that each of them aims to deliver the suffering patient from his sickness. In the same way, all religious teachings and methods are similar in that they are intended to free living beings from misery and the cause of misery, and to provide them with happiness and the cause of happiness. To cite a very famous verse from ancient India:

> By not committing any evil,
> By accomplishing every goodness,
> To subdue one's own mind absolutely—
> That is the teaching of the Buddha.

Until recently, the people in my Land of Snowy Mountains were left in complete isolation from their religious fellows all over the world. Although in ancient times Buddhism and Buddhist culture were largely brought from India by the great pandits of India's classical age and the great Tibetan scholars and translators who studied under them, and there was in general a close connection between the two countries, in more recent times we were regrettably cut off from development in the modern world. Now that we have suffered the great national disaster of virtual genocide, as is universally known, we can no longer doubt the impracticability of isolationism in modern times.

Nowadays the world is becoming increasingly materialistic, and mankind is reaching towards the very zenith of external progress, driven by an insatiable desire for power and vast possessions. Yet by this vain striving for perfection in a world where everything is relative, they wander ever further away from inward peace and happiness of the mind. This we can all bear witness to, living as we do plagued by unremitting anxiety in this dreadful epoch of mammoth weapons. It becomes more and more imperative that the life of the spirit be avowed as the only firm basis upon which to establish happiness and peace.

Therefore I pray that the precious light of the spirit will reign in the world for a long time, dispelling the dark shadows of materialism. It is imperative for all of us to resolve to make great efforts to hold its essence steadfastly in our hearts, and thence to disseminate it all over the world, opening the minds and hearts of all to its healing power. In so resolving, we eschew the path of mundane power, for the healing power of the spirit naturally follows the path of the spirit; it abides not in the stone of fine buildings, nor in the gold of images, nor in the silk from which robes are fashioned, nor even in the paper of holy writ, but in the ineffable substance of the mind and the heart of man. We are free to follow its dictates as laid down by the great teachers to sublimate our heart's instincts and purify our thoughts. Through actual practice in his daily life, man well fulfils the aim of all religion, whatever his denomination. And when the inner radiance generated by the practice of spirituality comes to light up the world again, as it has done in certain eras in the past, the masses who comprise the great nations of the world may take their inspiration from the Bodhi-mind of love and mercy, may relinquish their obsession with the vain pursuit of power, and may take refuge in the discipline of religion, the inexhaustible source of blessing, the universal panacea.

Part Six: The Two Truths

Buddhism has flourished in Tibet for over 1,000 years. During these centuries it has been carefully preserved and has become the basis of our culture. Nevertheless, although our culture has been nourished by many things of worth from neighbouring countries, we have on the whole been very much on our own.

In Tibet we practised Buddhism in its entirety. In garb and conduct, the monks practised according to the rules of the Vinaya Sutras; in the training of mind, we followed the Mahayana philosophy; and we also practised Tantric Buddhism. That is why I have used the phrase 'in its entirety'. Today, however, we are passing through a period of unimaginable difficulty and hardship.

The world today is engulfed in conflicts and sufferings to such an extent that everyone longs for peace and happiness; that longing has unfortunately led them to be carried away by the pursuit of ephemeral pleasure. But there are a few learned people who, dissatisfied by what is ordinarily seen or experienced, think more deeply and search for true happiness. I believe that the search will continue. As we make greater material progress and are able to satisfy our daily needs more fully, man will continue to search for Truth, not being satisfied with material progress alone. Indeed, I am convinced that the search for Truth will grow even keener.

In past centuries, there have been many learned teachers who have laid down various paths to the realisation of Truth. Among them, Lord Buddha is one, and my study of Buddhism has led me to form the opinion that, despite the differences in the names and forms used by the various religions, the ultimate truth to which they point is the same.

In Buddhism we have relative truth and absolute truth. From the viewpoint of absolute truth, what we feel and experience in our ordinary daily life is all delusion. Of the various delusions, the sense of discrimination between oneself and others is the worst form, as it creates nothing but unpleasantness for both sides. If we can realise and meditate on ultimate truth, it will cleanse our impurities of mind and thus eradicate the sense of discrimination. This will help to create true love for one another. The search for ultimate truth is, therefore, vitally important.

In the search for ultimate truth, if it fails to dawn on us it is we who have not found it. Ultimate truth exists. If we think deeply and reflect carefully, we shall realise that we ourselves have our existence in ultimate truth. For example, I am talking to you and you are listening to me. We are generally under the impression that there is a speaker and an audience and that there is the sound of words being spoken but, in ultimate truth, if I search for myself I will not find it, and if you search for yourselves you will not find them. Neither speaker nor audience, neither words nor sound, can be found. They are all void like empty space. Yet they are not completely non-existent. They must exist, for we are able to feel them. What I am saying is being heard by you, and you are in turn thinking on the subject. My speech is producing some effect, yet if we search for them we cannot find them. This mystery relates to the dual nature of truth.

Anything whose existence is directly perceivable by us can be classified as pertaining to relative truth. But, in ultimate truth, neither the searcher nor the object being searched for exists. Ultimate truth is void like empty space, beyond every form of obstruction and complication. Once we understand this, we can achieve true mental peace. It is my hope that, as the world becomes smaller and smaller owing to material progress and better communications we shall, as a result, all be able to understand more about ultimate truth. When this happens, I have great hope that we shall achieve true world peace.

Part Seven: The Three Higher Trainings

THE HIGHER TRAINING IN DISCIPLINE

No matter what form of Buddhism one wishes to practise—Hinayana, Mahayana, or Vajrayana—one must begin by cultivating the Three Higher Trainings. Buddha Shakyamuni himself, whose nature was compassion aspiring only to benefit beings and who possessed the boundless and inconceivable jewel-like qualities of a Sugata's three special transcendences and insights, completed the path and taught in this way.

The doctrine that he taught is of two types: the transmission of words or the scriptures, and the transmission of insight. The latter refers to the inner accomplishment of the Three Higher Trainings: self-discipline, meditative concentration and wisdom. In the Hinayana one practises these on the basis of renunciation and the aspiration to gain personal nirvana; in the Mahayana they are practised on the basis of and with the motivation to fulfil the vast Bodhisattva aspiration of gaining full Buddhahood in order to be of maximum benefit to the world.

The first of these, the higher training in self-discipline, is said to be the basis of the other trainings and the foundations of all perfections. The Buddha himself said: "Just as the earth is the basis of life and gives birth to all that grows, likewise, discipline is the basis of those making spiritual endeavour and it gives birth to every virtue."

Also it is said in *The Great Sutra on the Entering into Parinirvana:* "Discipline is the staircase leading to every wholesome truth. Like the earth which is the basis for the growth of the trees and so forth that live upon it, discipline is the basis of all spiritual progress. Just as a chief of merchants moves in front of all other merchants, it moves before all other wholesome Dharmas. Like the victory banner of Indra which flies above that of all other gods, it is the victory banner of all truth and cuts off the path leading to evil and to miserable states of being."

The practice of discipline is advocated by all sects of Tibetan Buddhism. The great Sakya Lama Drakpa Gyaltsen wrote, "If self-discipline is learned from the beginning, one possesses the root of higher being, a stepladder for achieving spiritual liberation, and an antidote eliminating misery and sorrow. Without discipline no method is effective."

The incomparable Kargyupa master Dvakpo (i.e. Gampopa), wrote in his *lam-rim* treatise, *The Jewel Ornament of Liberation,* "If one does not possess self-discipline, one will not gain liberation from the three worlds of samsara. As the path to Buddhahood is not complete, full and perfect enlightenment cannot be attained. Conversely, if one possesses self-discipline, one lays the foundations of every goodness and joy. It is like the fertile earth, and by relying upon it, the harvest of every perfection is increased."

Moreover, the omniscient Nyingma master Long Chen Rabjampa states in his *A Treasury of Oral Teachings*, "The root of the doctrine is known as discipline, and not to guard discipline leads to evil. Without the resolution to protect oneself, the root of one's Dharma practice soon will rot. Discipline is to be understood as the basis of every perfection, a ladder leading to higher being, a mount on which to ride to liberation. Therefore, make every effort to cherish the guarding of self-discipline."

Finally, the mighty Lama Jamgon Tsong Khapa also wrote, "Ethical discipline is water to clean away the stains of evil, moonlight to cool the heat of delusion, radiance towering like a mountain in the midst of sentient beings, the force peacefully to unite mankind. Knowing this, spiritual aspirants guard it as they would their very eyes. I, a yogi, practised like that. You, O liberation seeker, should do likewise."

Thus we can see the value placed upon the practice of discipline by all the learned and accomplished teachers of both India and Tibet's snowy mountains.

Discipline is a supreme ornament and, whether worn by old, young or middle aged people, gives birth only to happiness. It is perfume *par excellence* and, unlike ordinary perfumes which travel only with the wind, its refreshing aroma travels spontaneously in all directions. A peerless ointment, it brings relief from the hot pains of delusion.

Even if one does not possess the ordination of a monk, the practice of self-discipline transports one above the ranks of the masses. The master Acharya Vira wrote, "To attain the special path of discipline is to attain equality with those having instincts of compassion. Discipline, sharing the nature of immaculate wisdom, is a supreme ornament free of every defect.

"A monk should not wear ordinary perfumes, but discipline is the sweetest perfume found anywhere within the three worlds; and wearing it does not transgress a monk's trainings.

"Even if one is not a monk but leads the life of a layman, if one possesses self-discipline one becomes superior to ordinary men."

Especially in this degenerate age it is more beneficial to maintain the practice of discipline than it is to worship the Buddhas of the three times persistently in six sessions during the day and night. The practice of discipline in the present times surpasses that of all four complete trainings in previous ages. To guard merely one vow in the present age when the doctrine of Buddha has greatly degenerated in purity and strength is more beneficial than maintaining all disciplines in previous times. This was stated in *The King of Absorption Sutra*: "With a mind absorbed in the purity of devotion to honour billions of Buddhas for aeons equal to the sands of the Ganges with offerings of foods, drinks, umbrellas, flags and strings of butter lamps; or in this present age when the doctrine of the Tathagata is subsiding and the practice of Dharma coming to an end, to guard one's precepts day and night: the latter produces the greater merit."

In brief, by means of observing the essential points of elimination and cultivation precisely as specified by the mighty and transcended Buddha one undoubtedly will come into harmony with all beings treading the spiritual path.

On the other hand, to take a discipline upon oneself and then not to protect it, and to transgress the limits of the discipline, produces many undesirable effects. If in this world one transgresses the laws of a powerful ruler, there is a chance that one may nonetheless escape punishment by some means of good fortune. However, Buddha was not a mere political ruler, and the disciplines that he taught for his disciples were not given without reason, cause or purpose. Knowing well the vital necessity of the teachings on avoiding physically harming oneself as well as others, the precious value of knowing pure Dharma and the beneficial effects of the practice of self-discipline, the Buddha Shakyamuni gave the various precepts on what is to be eliminated and what cultivated. Therefore to transgress the precepts of enlightenment is not the same as transgressing a ruler's law, which sometimes results in one's downfall and sometimes not. The effects of a transgression of discipline will definitely ripen one day in the form of suffering.

The King of Absorption Sutra states: "If the legs of one's discipline are weak, one will not be able to travel to the city of liberation. Those with weak discipline will continue to wander in cyclic existence and will be crushed by the heavy sufferings of birth, old age, sickness and death."

Not only will these detrimental effects be produced by the degeneration of one's discipline; in addition it is said that if one's discipline becomes weakened, then even if one enters into the practices of Highest Tantra, none of the attainments described in the Tantric scriptures will be achieved. *The Root Tantra of Manjushri* states: "Buddha did not say that those who trangress their discipline will attain Tantric *Siddhi*. The transgression of discipline is not in the place or direction of nirvana. How can the great Tantric attainments come to naughty children unable to attain simple precepts? How can they even gain a happy rebirth? They will not evolve to higher being, nor will they attain everlasting joy. Why bother to speak of their vain hopes for gaining the attainments described in the Tantric methods taught by Buddha?"

Such are the faults of allowing one's disciplines to degenerate as described extensively in scriptures. Those wishing to attain happiness should therefore guard whatever disciplines they have taken upon themselves as diligently as they would guard their eyes.

To fulfil one's disciplines one must cultivate the five conditions. The first of these deals with the external condition of observing discipline through relying upon a spiritual preceptor. This means that one should thoroughly study the points of training as explained in the scriptures, not by personal reading but through hearing them from qualified teachers. Then, having gained clear understanding of the precepts, one should guard them precisely as taught.

Second is the inner condition of observing one's discipline through relying upon an excellent motivation. This means the firm resolution to maintain mindfulness of the precepts in every situation of daily life, whether moving, walking, lying down or sitting, and to maintain these precepts perfectly.

The third thesis is how to observe one's discipline by means of recognising the factors contradicting the precepts. To a fully ordained *Bhikshu* this entails thoroughly knowing the 253 precepts of his training, and understanding precisely what transgresses each. To a layman it means observing the refuge precepts, 10 disciplines and whatever of the five lay vows have been taken.

The fourth condition relates to how to protect one's discipline by means of strict observance of all precepts one has taken. The fifth concerns protecting one's discipline by means of relying upon the condition of abiding in joy. Both of these subjects should be learned from more detailed scriptures.

Once one has taken any precepts, one should practise so as to avoid staining one's stream of being with even the subtlest blot of transgression.

The compassionate Buddha himself said: "For some, discipline is joy; for others, it is misery. Maintaining discipline produces joy, breaking one's discipline leads to misery."

As stated by the master, it is extremely important to guard one's discipline. Moreover, in order to abide within pure discipline one must be aware of the four doors through which the downfalls make their entrance, and must seal off these entrances.

The first of the four entrances is ignorance. As explained earlier, the remedy to this is to cultivate an effective relationship with a spiritual teacher and study the points of training, thus becoming learned in the subjects to be eliminated and cultivated.

The second entrance is disrespectfulness. Its remedy is to abide within respectful thought toward Buddha, his teachings and the Dharma friends who dwell within pure ways.

The third entrance is mindlessness. Its remedy is to rely upon mindfulness which does not forget the points of practice, and to rely upon alertness, modesty and consideration. By not becoming separated from these forces and by continually examining the flow of one's body, speech and mind, the entrance of transgression and downfall is cut off.

The fourth entrance is the host of delusions and afflicted emotions. The remedy is to recognise whatever delusion is predominant and to eliminate it with its specific meditative antidote. For example, lust is to be counteracted by meditation upon ugliness; anger by meditation upon love; pride by meditation upon the various realms of the world; confusion by meditation upon interdependent origination, and so forth. One should strive in this way to watch for the arisal of delusion, and by relying upon the specific opponents to keep one's mindstream from falling under the power of delusion.

Should the forces of ignorance, mindlessness, etc. cause one to become stained by a downfall, one should immediately recognise the situation and as described should apply the four opponent forces with a mind of regret and resolution. One should not live with an unpurified downfall for even a day.

Should one leave a downfall or transgression unpurified, its negative effect is said to double in strength every day. Therefore one should take care to guard one's discipline and immediately to purify any stain that arises.

What are the immediate benefits of guarding precepts of discipline? The main function of discipline in terms of immediately beneficial effects is that it eliminates fallacious activity of body and speech and consequently one experiences pacification of coarse mental wandering to external objects, such as distraction by meaningless endeavours like overcoming enemies and protecting friends. Thus in this very life one gains the beneficial effect of abiding within inner joy. Through constantly possessing mindfulness and by the power of relying upon awareness of the points of practice together with alertness, the power of samadhi is easily and quickly attained.

The Higher Training In Meditative Concentration

The second of the Three Higher Trainings is meditative concentration, or samadhi. Discipline is the supreme fountainhead for the accomplishment of samadhi. In reliance upon the pacification of coarse mental wandering to external objects through the practice of discipline, one is spontaneously led to the sphere of thought prepared to engage in the cultivation of purely focused absorption. At that time one applies the methods of pacifying the subtle inner mental wanderings, such as subtle torpor and excitation, and can accomplish samatha, the essence of the training in samadhi. When this has been accomplished one experiences the beneficial effects of being able to meditate with great strength upon any of the spiritual subjects constituting the path to higher being and enlightenment, without being distracted by subjects other than those being meditated upon. Therefore, one should strive to accomplish samatha.

As a preliminary to the actual methods of accomplishing samatha one should abide within pure discipline while living in a solitary place conducive to mental peace. One should avoid associating with many people and eliminate the coarse conceptual mind of attraction to the objects of sensory experience.

The actual method of developing samatha is to adopt an object of concentration and pursue the process to completion. There are several types of subjects that may be used as the object of concentration: a pervasive object, an object of analytical thought, an object of wisdom, an object of purified delusion and so forth. A simple yet effective object commonly used these days is the image of the Tathagata.

One sits with legs crossed into the vajra posture, one's hands fixed in the meditation posture, back held straight, teeth and lips relaxed in a natural manner, one's tongue against the palate, head slightly inclined, eyes at the level of the point of the nose, and the shoulders erect. The body is held in this way, while internally one fixes one-pointedly upon a visualisation of an object such as an image of Buddha Shakyamuni. As one meditates, one relies upon the eight antidotes for eliminating the five faults and shortcomings.

In the beginning the main problem obstructing the progress of samadhi is laziness. There are four antidotes to be applied: faith which arises as a result of seeing the beneficial effects of samadhi; the motivation of interest in developing samadhi; enthusiastic perseverance in the methods of samadhi; and the ecstasy which is the result of persevering in training.

Once concentration has begun, the main obstacle is unawareness which loses the image upon which concentration is being directed. To remedy this, one single-pointedly concentrates upon the object while maintaining sharpness of mind and clarity of the visualised object.

When absorbed in the practice of concentration, the two main obstacles to progress are mental torpor and excitation. The remedy is to meditate while continually examining whether or not either of these two problems has arisen. Should either of them arise, one must immediately recognise them with the force of alertness.

The main obstruction hindering the birth of pure samadhi in the initial stages of practice is mental cloudiness which produces a sleeplike situation, such as a sense of physical heaviness and unclarity in the visualisation. Even though the visualisation may be clear and stable, it has no radiance of appearance. This is coarse torpor and its occurrence is like a dark mist falling over the mind. On the other hand, the object may appear with radiance but perhaps one will not have much sustaining power. This is subtle torpor and it is like a rope tied too loosely.

The next obstacle is mental excitation, such as mentally wandering to pleasant thoughts or images. Then there is the obstacle of not applying the opponents to these, the remedy for which is to rely upon an attitude of applying the meditative antidotes whenever the obstacles arise.

Should one practise in this way and yet, even though there is not even subtle torpor or excitement, one does not abide within an unbroken stream of single-pointed concentration, this is the fifth obstacle: that of over-application of the opponent forces. The remedy at that time is to abide calmly without applying antidotes, refraining from strongly exerting alertness and generally relaxing tension internally and externally.

Should one successfully practise with skilful means the ways of protecting one's progress from the obstacles, eventually one attains the signs of accomplishment of samadhi together with a blissful pliancy of body and mind.

The above explanation of the methods for developing samatha and samadhi is but a brief account. To actually develop samadhi one must understand the methods of accomplishing the nine stages of mental fixation by means of the six powers as described in the scriptures of the early Indian Buddhist masters. One should also receive teaching from the mouth of an experienced spiritual teacher.

THE HIGHER TRAINING IN WISDOM

Should one attain the non-conceptual blissfully clear absorption able to focus single-pointedly upon any subject of meditation for as long as desired, not only will one be able to meditate without distraction, one's powers of spiritual inquiry will gain unprecedented strength. One should then use this new power to engage in the training of wisdom which investigates the egoless nature of the objects of knowledge and realises the point of spiritual investigation.

The reason for engaging in the wisdom training is that mere accomplishment of samadhi devoid of training in wisdom which perceives the egoless nature of every phenomenon is not a method able to uproot the delusions and afflicted emotions such as ego-grasping, the source of cyclic existence. Even if one were to abide in samadhi for an aeon, unless it is conjoined with wisdom one will not attain the state of liberation. Consequently one must definitely cultivate the wisdom understanding egolessness. This is the remedy to eliminate all the delusions.

In the initial stages of the process of cultivating wisdom it is most important to recognise how the false 'I' arises. This is the 'I' to be eliminated by the wisdom of egolessness.

The nature of the 'I' to be eliminated and the way of experiencing the wisdom of egolessness to be cultivated has various modes of explanation in accordance with the viewpoint of the four schools of Buddhist thought.

The above process for the Hinayana path begins with contemplation of the general and specific shortcomings of samsara. This gives birth in one's mindstream to an unfeigned interest in gaining liberation from samsara. The Sravaka or Pratyekabuddha practitioners, in order to attain their individual states of enlightenment, then mainly engage in study and contemplation of the teachings. Firstly they accomplish the paths of accumulation, in which one endeavours to apply oneself to the collection of spiritual goodness.

Then if one can attain the wisdom able to meditate upon samatha and vipasyana combined and gain an understanding of egolessness, one attains the path of application. Thirdly, if by means of single-pointed meditation upon the meaning of egolessness one can gain direct insight into 'only-thatness', the Dharmadhatu equal to space, one attains the path of insight. Then by means of a sustained wisdom on the point of egolessness one gradually eliminates the great and small delusions to be abandoned by the path of meditation. Eventually, by means of the Vajra-like absorption of the path of meditation, one forever abandons even the most subtle delusions and attains one's specific state of Arhantship (i.e. either Sravaka or Pratyekabuddha).

In the Mahayana the motivation is more vast, as it takes as its basis the altruistic Bodhi-mind which cherishes others more than self, together with the vast activities that arise from this motivation, such as the six or 10 perfections. Through practice of these one progressively transcends the paths of accumulation and preparation, eventually gaining direct insight into emptiness. This marks the unobstructed path of insight and the first Arya Bodhisattva level, the path of liberation, thus eliminating all the obstacles of the path of liberation together with the syndrome of grasping at true existence. At that time one's practice of generosity, the first of the 10 perfections, gains special strength. Gradually one ascends through the remaining nine Bodhisattva levels, each of which is marked by the gaining of special strength in each of the remaining nine perfections.

On the first seven Bodhisattva levels, which are called 'the impure levels', one gradually abandons all the medium and great obstacles to the path of meditation of the three worlds and nine systems. Then on the eighth Bodhisattva level one simultaneously eliminates the subtle obstacles to the path of meditation. From this time onward the main obstacle becomes the obscurations to omniscience. At the end of training in this path one gains the last stage of the path, which counteracts the most subtle obstacles to omniscient wisdom able to perceive without hindrance all objects of knowledge.

Part Eight: Love and Compassion

In our approach to life, be it pragmatic or otherwise, a basic fact that confronts us squarely and unmistakably is the desire for peace, security and happiness. Different forms of life at different levels of existence make up the teeming denizens of this earth of ours. And, no matter whether they belong to the higher groups such as human beings or to the lower groups such as animals, all beings primarily seek peace, comfort and security. Life is as dear to a mute creature as it is to a man. Even the lowliest insect strives for protection against dangers that threaten its life. Just as each one of us wants happiness and fears pain, just as each one of us wants to live and not to die, so do all other creatures.

The faculty of reasoning, the ability to think and the power of expression distinguish man as a being superior to his mute friends. In the quest for peace, comfort and security, the methods applied by man are diverse and, sometimes, radically opposed to one another. All too frequently, the means adopted are cruel and revolting. Behaving in a way that is utterly unbecoming to his human status, man indulges in inhumane cruelties, torturing his fellow men as well as members of the animal kingdom just for the sake of selfish gain; such behaviour has almost become the order of the day. Such unskilled actions bring suffering to oneself as well as to others. Having been born as human beings, it is vitally important for us to practise benevolence and perform meritorious deeds for ourselves and others in this life and in lives to come. To be born a human being is a rare experience, and it is wise to use this golden opportunity as effectively and skilfully as possible.

Buddhism, with its emphasis on universal love and compassion impregnated with ideas that are wholly non-violent and peaceful, offers a means, at once unique and eternal, for the successful attainment of that state of security and happiness from which man and beast can derive common benefit. It can rightly be asserted that loving-kindness and compassion are the two corner stones on which the whole edifice of Buddhism stands. Destruction or injury to life is strictly forbidden. Harming or destroying any being from the highest to the lowest, from a human to the tiniest insect, must at all costs be avoided. The Blessed One said: "Do not harm others. Just as you feel affection on seeing a dearly beloved person, so should you extend loving-kindness to all creatures." Those who follow the Mahayanist way are admonished not only to abstain from doing injury but also to cultivate a great spirit of compassion involving an eager longing to save all sentient beings from pain and misery.

The arising of mahakaruna in the mind will prepare the ground for the perfect fruition of the precious Bodhi-mind, which is a necessary condition for attaining the supreme status of a Bodhisattva. One is called a Bodhisattva when one's mind is filled with the pure compassion and equanimity which proceed from Bodhi-mind. As whatever we do in our everyday life results from the functioning of our minds, ultimate peace and Buddhahood are the result of Bodhi-mind and compassion. The Lord Buddha has said: "Bodhi-mind is the seed of all Dharmas." Acharya Nagarjuna said: "If you wish to acquire the supreme status of a Bodhisattva, you must cultivate the quality of Bodhi-mind which should be as firm as a rocky mountain." Another Buddhist scholar, Acharya Chandrakirti, wrote: "In the beginning, mahakaruna (boundless compassion) is like a seed; it becomes as water and manure in the middle, and as ripe fruit at the end." All these sayings emphasise the matchless efficacy of Bodhi-mind. The intention to do good to others, the persistent thought in our hearts for the welfare of others, will spontaneously create happiness among the people around us. To return good for evil, benevolence for injury, love for hate, and compassion for harm, are some of the characteristics of the quality of Bodhi-mind. Deeds of benevolence and loving-kindness, not responding to ill-will from the other side, will delight the hearts of all. Indulgence in resentment and vengeance will only increase miseries to ourselves and others in this life and in lives to come.

Whatever method is adopted for the cultivation of the quality of Bodhi-mind, the fact remains that the birth-cycles of all sentient beings are beginningless, and that numberless times in previous lives we have each fulfilled the role of a mother. The feeling of a mother for her child is a classic example of love. For the safety, protection and welfare of her children, a mother is ready to sacrifice her very life. Recognising this, children should be grateful to their mothers and express their gratitude by performing virtuous deeds. In the same way, a person motivated by the thought of Bodhi-mind strives with all his might for the welfare of every sentient being, whether it be a human or a beast or a creature of land or sea. At the same time, he will treat all beings as he treats his mother. In repayment of her maternal love, it will be his constant endeavour to do only what is benevolent. In short, the cultivation of compassion and loving-kindness for all sentient beings will bring peace and happiness to ourself and others. Ill-will, malice and malevolent acts will only be a source of suffering to all.

The noble aspiration to attain Buddhahood, to cultivate Bodhi-mind in thought and to practise charity, forbearance, morality, kindness and so on are all for the sake of living beings. It is for them that these ennobling and uplifting qualities are sought. The creatures that inhabit this earth—be they human beings or animals—are here to contribute, each in its own particular way, to the beauty and prosperity of the world. Many creatures have toiled singly or jointly to make our life comfortable. The food we eat, the clothes we wear, have not just dropped from the sky. Many creatures have laboured to produce them. That is why we should be grateful to all our fellow creatures. Compassion and loving kindness are the hallmarks of achievement and happiness. Let us practise them for the welfare of all.

Part Nine: The Bodhi-mind

All religions, in teaching moral precepts to mould the functions of mind, body and speech, have primarily the same noble goal. They all teach us not to lie or bear false witness, not to steal or take other's lives and so on. That there are so many different religions to bring happiness to mankind is analogous to the treatment of a particular disease by different methods. For, in the most general terms, all religions aim to help each living being to avoid misery and acquire happiness. Thus, although we can find causes for preferring individual interpretations of religious truth, there is much greater cause for unity stemming from the heart. In the present state of the world, the need to evolve a great measure of unity among the followers of the different religions has become especially important. Moreover, such unity is not an impossible ideal.

Bodhi-mind forms the central theme of Mahayana Buddhism in Tibet. We believe that the concept of Bodhi-mind will go a long way in helping to achieve basic unity and a spirit of co-operation among the followers of different creeds. We believe that striving in itself will effect great results. The Blessed One acquired Bodhi-mind after making innumerable sacrifices and powerfully concentrated efforts. For three immeasurable aeons he practised the deeds of a Bodhisattva, making unstinting sacrifices and undergoing great hardships, thus gradually acquiring the dual accumulations of merit and wisdom. Finally, at Buddha Gaya, he attained to the supreme enlightenment which is called Buddhahood. Emancipated from the misery that follows clinging to the extremes of the mundane and the sublime, he reached that perfect equanimity that flows from the ultimate ineffable peace called nirvana, free of every fault. His intellect perfected beyond the minutest error or illusion, he proceeded to evolve the many forms of the Holy Dharma, turning the Threefold Wheel of the Dharma in accordance with the system of the Four Noble Truths and of Interdependent Origination, all in revelation of the dual truth (relative and absolute).

The inspiration to achieve this ineffable Bodhi-mind can be expressed in this way: "I must attain the supreme state of omniscient Buddhahood, so that I can liberate all sentient beings from this ocean of misery, samsara, and establish them in the ultimate happiness of nirvana."

This inspiration creates a longing to devote one's energy to both the profound and extensive stages of the path of Mahayana. It is the root of the practice for accomplishing the Bodhisattva deeds, which connotes generosity, morality, patience, perseverance, meditation and wisdom. To be more precise, from the first three—generosity, morality and patience—stem the accumulation of virtue. From the last two—meditation and wisdom—stem the accumulation of sublime wisdom. And the fourth one, perseverance, leads to both accumulations. In short, the key to the practice of Mahayana Buddhism in Tibet is dual co-ordination at every level, the co-ordination of virtue and wisdom, method and knowledge, Tantra and Sutra, relative and absolute. Simultaneously, careful attention must be paid to the inherent moral implications of all the Buddha's teachings, i.e. desisting from harming others and cultivating the spirit of loving-kindness. Viewed from the perspective of Bodhi-mind, the goal is to maintain undiscriminating compassion towards all living beings without making any distinction of race, nationality, class or the tenuous status of friend or enemy. In time, the great nations of the world, inspired by Bodhi-mind, may cease to manipulate everything, both sacred and profane, in a vain pursuit of power, and instead try to create a peaceful world by regulating the mind's activities to accord with Dharma, the inexhaustible treasure.

Part Ten: Buddhadharma and Society

For many centuries man has been talking about justice, harmony and peace. In these modern days of material abundance and stupendous advancement in science and technology it seems that the more sophisticated our lives become, the less we seem to be conscious of these high ideals. And yet, there is no doubt about the need for these, for without them the very survival of human society is at stake. As followers of Buddhadharma we must make our contributions towards the realisation of these.

The achievement of justice, harmony and peace depends on many factors. I would like to think about them in terms of human benefit—in the long run rather than for the short term. I realise the difficulty of the task before us. But we have no alternative. The world has shrunk and has become more interdependent than ever before. Nations have no choice but to be concerned about the welfare of others, not only because of their belief in humanity, but because it is in their self-interest. Under the circumstances, there is definitely a growing need for human understanding, and a sense of universal responsibility. The key to the achievement of these high ideals lies in generating a good and kind heart. For, unless we develop a feeling of humaneness, we can neither hope to achieve universal happiness nor lasting peace.

I believe in the need for human understanding and harmony for a wider reason, which is simply that we are all human beings. Geographical, cultural and physical differences are superficial. Even differences of faith and ideology are transcended when we begin to think of ourselves as human beings. We all want happiness and do not want suffering, and every human being has the right to pursue happiness. For in the final analysis, all of us basically have the same hopes and aspirations, and all of us belong to the same human family.

Buddhism is one of the many religions which teaches us to be less selfish and more compassionate. It teaches us to be humane, altruistic and to think of others in the way we think of ourselves. Our daily thoughts and actions should be directed towards the benefit of others. Mahayana emphasises self-sacrifice and the development of altruism, while Hinayana teaches us the importance of not harming others. The practice of

81

Buddhism in essence is, therefore, not to harm others under any circumstances, and to help others as much as possible.

By living in a society we should share the sufferings of our fellow beings and practise compassion and tolerance, not only towards our loved ones but also towards our enemies. This is the test of our strength and practice, as emphasised by Mahayana. Unless we can set an example by our own practice we cannot hope to convince others of the value of Dharma by mere words. We should engage in the same high standards of integrity and sacrifice that we ask of others. The ultimate purpose of Buddhism, and for that matter all religions, is to serve and benefit man. That is why it is of the utmost importance for us to ensure that Buddhism is always employed to realise the happiness and peace of man and not to convert others or to derive benefit from them.

In this ever-changing world there are two important things that Buddhists should keep in mind. The first is self- examination. We should re-examine our own attitude towards others and constantly check ourselves to see whether we are practising properly. Before pointing our finger at others we should point it towards ourselves. Secondly, we must be prepared to admit our faults and stand corrected.

There is no doubt that the Buddhadharma is faultless; but over the centuries as it was practised in many parts of the world—including my country till about two decades ago—social and traditional influences have crept into it. We should after careful examination be prepared to correct and weed these out when they are no longer beneficial or relevant.

The Buddha's teachings consist of Hinayana and Mahayana, and of Tantrayana, which is an important part of Mahayana. Much incorrectly ascribed information and a lack of appreciation and proper understanding of the deeper significances of these paths have led to many false impressions and misconceptions about them. I would, therefore, like to say something about the way these teachings were studied and practised in Tibet, in the hope that it will help to create a better comprehension of them.

During his own lifetime, Shakyamuni Buddha gave many discourses and instructions, from which later arose the four schools of Buddhist tenets, namely, Vaibhasika, Sautrantika, Chittamatra and Madhyamaka, and the two systems of practice and experience, Sravaka Pratyeka-buddhayana and Bodhisattvayana. In Tibet all these teachings were studied and practised thoroughly and with great devotion. Though it was the Madhyamaka tenets that Tibetan Buddhists finally settled for, they in no way looked down upon the other schools and, in fact, studied their tenets with equal enthusiasm and interest, as the most effective means of understanding and realising the deeper significances of the upper schools. Even their conduct and discipline patterns were governed by the directions of the Vinaya, a Hinayana tradition, the teachings of which are regarded as the basis of all Buddhist practices. Hinayana consists of four major orders—Mahasamghika, Sarvastivada, Sthavira and Sammitiya—which are subdivided into 18 sects. Today only two of these four orders, Sarvastivada and Sthavira, exist.

Tibetans practise the Vinaya according to the Sarvastivadin tradition, while a number of countries like Sri Lanka follow the Sthavira tradition. There are no major differences between the two and they only vary in terms of enumeration, and commission and omission of minor rules. For instance, according to the Sarvastivadin tradition, Bhikshus are required to observe 253 vows, while according to the Sthavira tradition they are only required to keep 227 vows. Similarly, there is a slight difference in the number of Bhikshu downfalls/vows (*suddha-prayascihika*) as the Sarvastivadins have 90 while the Sthaviras have 92 vows. However, there is no such variation regarding the major vows of defeats (*parajika*). remainders (*samaghavasesa*) and forfeitures (*naihsargika payattika*).

As I have said before, Tibetan Buddhists not only have a deep respect for Hinayana but in their actual practice they try to integrate Hinayana observances in their conduct and day-to-day life, while internally they strive to develop Bodhi-mind, and to practise Tantrayana in secrecy.

Mahayana primarily seeks the state of Buddhahood for the sake of others. In conjunction with this aspiration, 16 aspects of the four truths such as impermanence and the 37 practices to enlightenment (*Bodhipaksika dharmas*), Mahayanists practise the six or 10 perfections (*paramitas*), and the four means of gathering disciples.

Vajrayana has four sets of Tantra: Kriya, Charya, Yoga and Anuttara-yoga, and is basically a path of practice where a practitioner tries to realise the subtle mind through the medium of developing a stabilised realisation of the union of samatha and vipasyana by concentrating on the various channels and the currents of energy of the body. Nowadays it seems to be attracting much interest and also many people seem to be stressing the similarities that exist between non-Buddhist and Buddhist Tantras to an extent of saying that they are both the same. I think this is a gross misconception and feel that one would understand Buddhist Tantra more clearly if one observes that mere similarities in certain practices do not justify the assertion of two systems as being the same. Otherwise, one would have to say that the Sutra teachings are the same as non-Buddhist teachings because both propound similar teachings with regard to certain practices and developments such as *dhyana* and *arupasamapttya*. Moreover, if one analyses carefully, one will find that the very basis upon which Tantrayana is founded is vastly different from those of non-Buddhist Tantra teachings, for Buddhist Tantrayana is based upon the fundamental teachings and realisation of Bodhi-mind and the theory of *anatma* (selflessness).

Efforts are also being made in various parts of the world for religious unity and for better understanding among the different faiths. It is indeed an important task, but we must remember that there is no quick and easy solution. We cannot hide the differences that exist among various faiths and neither can we hope to replace the existing faiths by a universal belief. Each religion has its own distinctive qualities and contributions to make, and each in its own way is suited to a particular group of people. For I believe that each of them basically aims at transforming man into a better and more decent human being. The world needs them all. Therefore I feel that if we want to achieve harmony and goodwill not only among followers of Buddhism but also among different religions, we must make every effort to create better understanding and more respect for one another's religions. Above all we must never use religion for selfish reasons such as to promote communal interests.

However difficult it may be for us to achieve these goals, I think we owe it to all mankind to make every effort. It is my hope that there will be a better understanding among Buddhists and, on a larger scale, a sense of universal responsibility and brotherhood between all spiritual traditions.

Part Eleven: Questions and Answers

Q: Your Holiness, here in Dharamsala and also on your visits to the West you have had considerable contact with Western people, who at present are showing a deep interest in the Tibetan spiritual traditions. Whenever the Buddhadharma has been absorbed into a new society, it has always been modified so as to have the greatest impact on the minds of the people. What can and what cannot be modified, particularly in the context of the Dharma in the West?

A: The fundamentals of the principal practices of Dharma ought not to be changed. For example, the bases of bodhicitta (the altruistic attitude of striving for Buddhahood as a means of benefitting all beings) and shunyata (emptiness, the ultimate nature of mind and of all things) will always be required by practitioners. However, in order to get at the essence of these practices, their secondary details—such as the sequential order of the ways in which they are approached, the specifics of the visualisations involved in them and so forth—might well be modified to accord with the differing mentalities of given people.

There were certain differences in the practices of ancient India and Tibet, yet the essential factors of bodhicitta, the core of the Mahayana, were identical. The differences were only in how bodhicitta was actualised. Even in India there were a number of approaches to it, such as "The Exchange of Self-cherishing for the Cherishing of Others", taught in Shantideva's "Venturing into the Deeds of a Bodhisattva" (Bodhisattva-caryavatara) and "The Method of Six Causes and One Effect", taught in Atisha's "Light on the Path" (Bodhipathapradipa). These different techniques were meant to suit different circumstances. Both aimed at developing the same bodhicitta and at outlining the practices of the Six Perfections.

Therefore, the details of various practices can differ to suit the Western mentality, and not only to suit the Western mentality in general but also to suit the individual practitioner's disposition.

Q. All the great masters have stressed the importance of having a spiritual teacher in order to avoid misunderstanding either the teachings or one's meditational experiences. Unfortunately, at present there are few teachers and many who wish to learn. Is it advisable for such a person to just read a meditation manual and then practise from it?

A. This is possible. Certain advanced meditations are dangerous if practised without the guidance of an experienced teacher, but simple meditations, such as those on impermanence, love, compassion or the development of samadhi, are good.

   Without a teacher, it is best to limit oneself to small and simple meditations.

Q. Many people wish to take up a spiritual practice but feel committed to devoting most of their time to job, family, etc. Is it possible to transform these concerns into sources of spirituality?

A. The major attitudes one needs in order to do this are kindness and bodhicitta.

   It is difficult to explain bodhicitta in brief and still be correct. Perhaps we can say that it is the motivation to help oneself so as to be able to help others. This profoundly kind attitude, bodhicitta, is the basis of all Mahayana teachings.

   To make ordinary activities spiritual, this attitude of kindness must be incorporated within every action of daily life. Certain meditations cannot be practised while you are working, for example in a factory, but meditation upon kindness and compassion can. If you sincerely try, Dharma can always be practised.

Q. The Buddhadharma as practised by Tibetans involves meditation upon a vast array of symbols and deities. Does Your Holiness see this as presenting any problems to the Western mind, with its monotheistic background?

A. This depends on the individual's character. Some people like these deities very much (laughter).

   Each person must think about what suits him best.

Q. Some say that these symbols and deities should be altered so as to correspond with those of our own culture.

A. This cannot be. If you follow Buddhadharma, the deities meditated upon should have a sound reference in the teachings of Buddha Vajradhara. They cannot be arbitrarily created nor can they be blended with those of other methods. It is best to follow with diligence the path most suited to you. If you choose Buddhadharma, practise it purely. Then, if you achieve its results, fine; if you mix practices and achieve nothing, you shouldn't blame Dharma.

Of the various Buddhist meditational deities, the best is Buddha. If you like others, practise them; if you don't, simply take Buddha.

Q. Is this 'liking' due to one's karmic dispositions?

A. It has to do with karmic dispositions. Buddhism speaks of idiosyncrasies, latent admirations and underlying tendencies, which together with one's intellect, circumstances and so forth constitute one's karmic dispositions. These are major factors determining which path one should follow.

Q. Many occidental translators of Tibetan texts lay great emphasis upon the external rather than the inner aspects of spiritual magic. How was this problem avoided in Tibet when the Tantric texts were translated from Sanskrit into Tibetan?

A. This does not seem to have been an excessively great problem in Tibet. However, there undoubtedly have been certain people who did not incorporate Dharma into their mental attitudes. In actuality, anyone who practises Tantric methods for such purposes as to destroy an enemy is not really a spiritual person. Whether or not a person is actually a spiritual practitioner is determined by the long-term benefits that his practice brings, not by the methods he uses.

Buddha Vajradhara taught Tantra to help beings attain enlightenment, not to give them an instrument for harming others. He always emphasised that Tantra is a secret doctrine, for in the hands of someone without the background of bodhicitta and other qualifications it can be dangerous and not at all beneficial.

The commentary to the "Root Text of Manjushri" (Manjushri Mula Tantra) tells a story of a Brahmin by the name of Kanaka, who was a practitioner of the Yamantaka Tantra. Although he was an extremely strong meditator with tremendous concentration and power, he fell into hell. His practice, meant to bring him enlightenment, only harmed him. In a commentary to the "Root Text of Guhyasamaja" (Guhyasamaja Mula Tantra) the same point is stressed.

Anything that has happened in Tibet along these lines is not good and any such interest elsewhere is the same.

The true Tantric practitioner has taken a commitment not to show whatever magical powers he may possess. According to the Vinaya rules, even if you are an Arhant you should not openly reveal your attainments to others. It is the same in Tantra; if with little reason you expose your powers, even though you have certain qualifications the basis of your practice will degenerate.

Q. Of all Buddhist practices, those of the Tantrayana have attracted the most attention among Westerners; and not the preliminary Tantric practices but the very advanced Completion Stage practices which involve meditation on chakras, nadis, consorts and so forth. What are the advantages and disadvantages of this interest and what are the preliminaries of Tantric practice?

A. It is very good that Westerners have this interest in the Completion Stage. However, it is of little value to perform these without first becoming proficient in the practices of the Development Stage, where samadhi is developed and one's attitude towards Tantra matured by means of meditation upon the mystic mandala. Furthermore, this interest should be based on the motivation to benefit all beings; a difficult prerequisite. Interest motivated by mere idle curiosity lacks the proper foundation.

Meditation upon the Completion Stage of Tantra can be extremely dangerous, perhaps bringing many types of sickness and even death to the unqualified practitioner. Medicines cannot cure a sickness arising from performing these practices incorrectly; the only antidote is the proper application of a specific meditation.

Q. In brief, what is the difference between Hindu and Buddhist Tantra?

A. To fully understand their differences is extremely difficult. However, in brief, there are differences in both action and philosophy. In terms of action, the Buddhist Tantra is based on the bodhicitta motivation, which the Hindu Tantra lacks. In terms of philosophy, Buddhist Tantra is based on the theory of anatma, or selflessness, whereas the Hindu is based on the theory of a truly existent self. Other yogas, such as breathing exercises, chakra and nadi practices, etc., have many similarities but subtle differences.

Q. As self-cherishing and ego-holding are forces which have been active since beginningless time, is it possible to set out upon a spiritual path without developing a negative egoism towards it, leading to sectarianism?

A. To avoid that, it is necessary to take care that your Dharma practice is really a Dharma practice. This way, although the power of familiarity with ego is great, its effects are not overwhelming. If you study

Dharma but do not actually apply it, your so-called spiritual activities can easily become directed at material gain, fame and so forth. In which case only egoism and such negativities as anger, attachment, sectarianism, etc. are developed. However, if each word of Dharma that you hear is used to cultivate your mind, then every single word brings only benefit and, no matter how much Dharma learning you amass, your learning will never go to the development of egoism.

The most important point is to be very careful in the beginning with your motivation in receiving a teaching or doing a practice. If this is done well, there is little danger.

Q. Buddha Shakyamuni once said in a Sutra that sectarianism has a karmic consequence more severe than killing a thousand Buddhas. Why is this so?

A. The essential purpose of the Buddhas giving teachings is to eliminate both mistaken states of mind and the experience of suffering. This is also the reason that they have worked to achieve enlightenment. The Buddhas' only motivation is to benefit others, which they fulfil by teaching; so despising any of their teachings is worse than despising the Buddhas. This is the implication of following one Dharma tradition while disparaging other traditions.

Furthermore, the Buddhas themselves respect all the traditions of the teachings, so for us not to do so is to despise all the Buddhas.

There are many ways to look at this Sutra quotation. What is the duty, so to speak, of a Buddha? Only to teach Dharma. And it is Dharma which has brought that Buddha to his state of attainment. Now, in Buddhadharma we do not accept the theory of a Creator; everything depends on oneself. The Buddhas cannot directly fulfil their wish to help beings, they can only do so through the medium of their teachings. We might say that they are handicapped. Therefore, the teachings that they give are more precious and important than they are themselves. Because of the varying capacities and inclinations of beings, the Buddhas have taught various methods of practice and philosophy. If we follow one of these and yet belittle others, we abandon the Dharma and consequently the Buddhas as well.

Q. Does Your Holiness think that the various world religions were founded by emanations of the Buddhas manifesting in accordance with mentalities of specific societies?

A. This is highly possible. The founder of any religion could be an emanation of a particular Buddha. It is for this very reason that we should treat all religions with deep respect.

Q. Then why do these different religions so often fight with one another?
A. This is a different matter. For a truly rèligious person there is never any basis for quarrel or dispute. Yet it is a fact that there have been so-called religious wars. However, the people involved in these were not practising religion but were merely using religion as an instrument of power. The actual motivation was selfish, not spiritual. Religious wars are not a question of contradictions between religions at all.

Leaving aside disparities between the doctrines of different religions, there are many ostensible contradictions within the teachings of Buddha. For example, for certain reasons to some people he taught that there is no truly existent self, whereas to others he taught that there is. So what is a Buddha's purpose in teaching? It is neither to boast nor to demonstrate how much he knows, but to benefit others. Also, he is not concerned with those of his generation alone but with many generations and different kinds of people. Therefore, his teachings must have many different levels of meaning, some often seemingly contradictory. Knowing this, there is never a valid reason for religious quarrels and disputes.

Q. How does Tibetan Buddhism interpret the value of religion?
A. The real objective of religion (Dharma) is to serve the functions of a protector—a source of refuge. A system which provides security makes for a utilitarian, functional religion. And yet, whatever and howsoever might be the external activities, behaviour and forms provided for by the system, it cannot be viewed as falling within the perspective of a functional religion if it fails to provide, even elementarily, a means of refuge or protection. A religion involves practice of methods and modes conducive to the realisation of serenity, discipline, joyous detachment, and self-control. It should be observed that normally it is through the inattentive body, speech and mind that all harmful and unethical factor-conditions are created. Therefore, it naturally presupposes that the pacification, training, and taming of the physical, mental, and verbal activities are of fundamental importance. To sum up, it is essential first of all to rectify, nullify, and put a stop to all physical misconduct (pertaining to body), followed by that of the speech. Rectification of the unwholesome physical and verbal actions is in itself a method for controlling the mind. As to the

method to be adopted for taming the mind, the entire ramifications of the present mental stains and faults, beginning from the most serious and ending in the subtlest, are to be fully eradicated. Regarding the manner of eradication, the objective can be achieved in two ways: one, energetic suppression of some of the more pronounced and evident defilements; and, two, progressive elimination of all mental defilements, gross or subtle; and ultimately by eradicating their very sources (seed or first cause) in such a way that these are rendered impotent even when coming in contact with their ripening conditions. Such a process of eradication is total and complete.

Q. What meaning is given to the concept of karma in Tibet?

A. Karma and its fruits can roughly be described as volitional action and its fruits, or moral or psychological cause and effect. Methods of explaining the true nature of karma and its fruits are diverse and many. A generalised description would be that all phenomena and objects are the results of causes. An effect is produced by a cause. Whether the result is good or bad depends upon the individual mind. A negative cause and effect is indestructible and irrevocable. Take the example of a plant sapling. The effect, plant sapling, comes into being because of its previous cause, i.e. the seed. The quality of an effect is dependent upon the quality of its corresponding cause. Similarly, pleasure and pain, or happiness and suffering, which are the lot of sentient beings, come from the individual's past causes— good or bad. It is all because of the operation of the inexorable law of cause and effect. The discovery that karma exists and is a fact and a reality, that it increases, that there is no fruit unless conditioned by karma, and that nothing can hide from karma, is a truth of great significance.

Q. The traditional scriptures speak of the Three Vehicles. Why did the Buddha teach three paths?

A. Although the scriptures do speak of Three Vehicles—the Hearer's Vehicle, the Solitary Realiser's Vehicle and the Bodhisattva Vehicle—the first two of these are counted as one, the Hinayana. The Bodhisattva Vehicle, or Mahayana, is subdivided into the "Causal Vehicle of the Practice of the Perfections" and the "Resultant Vehicle of the Practice of Tantra". Thus in Tibet we usually speak of the two vehicles, the Hinayana and the Mahayana.

There are many different ways to look at these two. First we'll consider them from the point of view of practice.

It is very important to have as an external basis the observance of the Vinaya, i.e. maintaining one of the four ordinations of a monk or nun, or either of the two ordinations of a lay person.

For a monk, the three foundations of practice should be followed: Rainy Season Retreat, Bi-monthly Purification and the Ceremony Ending Rainy Season Retreat. These are all Hinayana practices.

In addition to the above, one should take up the practices of compassion, bodhicitta and the conduct of the Six Perfections, which are Causal Mahayana.

One person can perform all these practices for the attainment of enlightenment: they do not obstruct one another or cause any constrictions within the practitioner. Therefore, one person can practise all of them without contradiction. With this approach there can be no basis for Hinayana disparaging Mahayana, Mahayana disparaging Hinayana, Sutrayana disparaging Tantra and so forth. Such is the relationship of the vehicles from the point of view of action.

From the point of view of philosophy, Buddhadharma can be divided into the Four Schools (Vaibashika, Sautrantrika, Yogachara and Madhyamaka) which all come from India. In one way these seem to be mutually exclusive. However, the purpose of seemingly conflicting teachings within the framework of Buddhist philosophy is to provide a graduated approach to the higher philosophies, leading to an ever greater, and eventually ultimate understanding. Therefore, none of the four schools of philosophy is to be abandoned.

In Tibet there are four major traditions: Nyingma, Sa-kya, Kagyu and Ge-lug. From the point of view of practice, they are all Mahayanists following the unity of Sutrayana and Tantrayana, as described above, on the basis of Hinayana. From the point of view of philosophy, they are all Madhyamikas (who train in accordance with the graduated philosophical stages explained above). They do not differ from the points of view of action or philosophy. Their differences are due to the time of their coming to Tibet, the different lineages of Lamas who have introduced them, the different emphasis on the various aspects of practice and the terminologies by which their teachings are transmitted. All four lead to Buddhahood. Therefore, it is absolutely wrong to say one is better than another, or to disparage any of them.

Q. What is the exact meaning of nirvana? There is considerable confusion about this in the West, the general idea being that it means annihilation.

A. Literally, liberation or salvation (Tibetan: thar-pa) means freedom from bondage. Beings are ensnared and bound by karma and delusion. When the unsatisfactoriness or *dukkha* resulting from the bondage of (volitional actions) karma and delusion, or the state of unsatisfactoriness experienced owing to related influences of karma and delusion, is eradicated and tranquilised, one dwells in the state known as liberation. It is true that the various schools of Buddhist thought differ in expounding the true nature and import of the term 'liberation'. However, broadly speaking, it can be interpreted as the destruction of or freedom from unsatisfactoriness and its cause, given rise to by one's karma and delusion and their resulting dominant influences. Destruction of or freedom from unsatisfactoriness and its causes is achieved and effected by the strength of one's inner efforts, i.e. exercise of counteracting forces; or by virtue of the attainment of the supreme wisdom that comprehends shunyata (emptiness).

The theory of shunyata or emptiness is common ground for all the four main schools of Buddhist thought. However, the most perfect and excellent description of the meaning of shunyata, profound and vast as it is, can be found only in the Madhyamaka school of Buddhist thought, which is regarded as the principal school among the four. The term shunyata or voidness does not mean that there is nothing, that nothing exists, like describing a flower called sky-flower that does not exist at all. Shunyata is attributeless, but implies that whatever is born of a cause exists; yet exists only in relation to or dependent upon something other than itself. Its origination is not origination in fact: that is shunya. Things are simply mental designations and nothing else. They are non-self-existing. All objects are shunya by nature. They are void. They are empty of permanent substance or self because they are non-self-existing, being dependent upon causes other than themselves. But this does not mean that objects do not exist at all.

The 'I' (self) is a denomination named in relation to the aggregates (groups of physical and mental properties dependent on grasping). It is generally believed that the 'I' (self) and aggregates each have their own separate existences. However, Buddhists recognise and identify the nature of the self ('I') and the aggregates as being related. The 'I' depends upon the aggregates for its existence. For instance, a chariot is the name given to its different parts collectively. Similarly, it is possible for us to speak of the self or 'I' only in relation to the aggregates. To quote the words of the Master: "A chariot is named as such in relation to the cohesive whole of its different parts. Likewise, a relative living being is just a name designated in relation to the collectiveness (cohesive whole) of the aggregates." All the four main schools of Buddhist thought freely subscribe to this point of view, in spite of the fact that the approach adopted by each school in explaining the nature of the conditioned 'I' is quite different. Of the four schools, Madhyamaka is reckoned to be the most important. Madhyamaka is again divided into two sub-schools: Prasangika and Sautantrika. According to the Prasangika subschool, the self or 'I' is a mere name as construed by comprehension. Just as the self is a mere name as construed by comprehension, all objects are mere names as construed by comprehension. All objects are non-self-existent, i.e. they do not have an existence of their own.

Q. What special relevance does Tibetan Buddhism have to the problems of the modern age?

A. The Buddha's teachings comprise methods for securing a continuous process of mind-development by translating the teachings into real practice in accordance with the needs and realities of life. For this, a proper understanding of the realities or facts of life, i.e. the nature of phenomena and objects as they really are, is necessary. Again, there are two aspects: first, knowledge of things and events which are beyond a man's comprehension (man's limited mind): second, knowledge of objects and phenomena which are within the grasp of the mind's comprehension. But, first of all, we must ask and find answers to the most relevant question as to what exactly is mind, what is its nature, how does it work and so on. Once this is known, the mind acquires the power to cognise the nature and working of phenomena, and of objects as they really are. The mind becomes broad and free, increases in the bounds of patience and forgiveness, with a parallel progress in deepening and broadening of the thinking faculties. Realisation of mental prowess such as I have outlined here will be of greatest service and benefit to humanity in the present century.

Q. Tibetans consider the Tantrayana to be the most powerful teaching of Buddha. Why is Tantric practice so effective?

A. Causally speaking, we people of this world already have a similitude capable of being developed into the three bodies of a Buddha. Our five senses or present physical form is the basis of the physically appearing Emanation Body of a Buddha. The subtle dream body, which is also the Intermediate State Body between life and death, is like the Enjoyment Body. In turn, the root of both of these is the Clear Light itself, which is capable of being developed into the actual enlightenment of the Buddha, his Truth Body. The uncommon feature of Tantra is to transform these three ordinary bodies into the bodies of a Buddha.

Now I will explain how this is actually done. The human body as a configuration of energy is made up of 72,000 channels, the currents of energy which travel through them and the essential drops or units of consciousness and energy conjoined which reside in the channels. By manipulating the essential drops within the channels by way of the currents, we undergo different levels or states of consciousness. The type of consciousness we now have based on our present configuration is one type, dream another, deep sleep another. Fainting, heavy fainting or coma or when the breath stops are all others. The final level of consciousness, Clear Light, is made manifest at the time of death. This is the strongest and subtlest. Unused, it serves as the basis for revolving the round of birth, old age, sickness and death. Once one understands the nature of cyclic existence, though, one can be free of it. The best of all preparations for this is an understanding now of the different types of consciousness through making use of the channels, drops and inner airs or energies.

Tantra is extremely dangerous. Without proper guidance it cannot be accomplished. Thus practised it will often lead to insanity or death.

Q. Could Your Holiness please comment on the controversy as to whether or not it is possible for a human being to change his physical form entirely from one lifetime to the next?

A. I am a Buddhist. I believe that a human being may take on the form of a lower being. Where we are born in the next life is not dependent on unwholesome activities and virtue. The basic thing is our own karmic force. That is the seed. The seed alone, however, is not sufficient—it must interact with water and soil. So similarly we have to think not only in terms of cause but also in terms of conditions. Basically it is very clear. The main material of our physical body comes from parents. But our mind, our self, does not. So this physical body is almost like a house or clothes—we change from time to time.

Q. Is it possible to define the nature of the entity which migrates from one lifetime to the next?

A. In Buddhism we believe, we accept that there is 'I'. Yet we do not accept that 'I' as being something permanent, something independent from the body and mind.

There are four different schools of thought in Buddhism regarding the nature of this entity. All four schools of thought refute the existence of 'I' as a permanent entity which is independent from the body and mind; all four schools of thought deny this.

Now for the positive side—that which is accepted. This explanation differs in the four schools, from among which I will speak about the two Mahayana schools: Chittamatra and Madhyamika.

First, according to the Chittamatrins there are two explanations. Within one school of the Chittamatrins 'I' is not labelled on the basis of form (of the body) at all, but is solely identified on the basis of consciousness. They maintain that there are eight different types of consciousness; the five sense consciousnesses, the sixth is mental consciousness, the seventh is a negative consciousness that takes as its object foundational consciousness and has a wrong appreciation of this foundational consciousness, and the eighth is foundational consciousness (*alayavijnana*) itself. Within this school they regard the eighth consciousness, foundational consciousness, as the 'I'.

Their reasoning is that when we die the five sense consciousnesses and mental consciousness cease to be active. Therefore unless the 'I' is identified as another consciousness apart from these six consciousnesses, the 'I' would not continue. There must be an 'I' and it must be something other than the six consciousnesses that cease to exist at death. So they maintain that there is another consciousness, which is accepted as 'I'.

That is one school. Within the other school of Chittamatrins they regard 'I' as the sixth mind, the mental consciousness itself. They accept only the six consciousnesses and the sixth consciousness is held to be 'I'.

Now here in the Madhyamika school of thought, again there is a division into two: the Svatantrika-Madhyamika and the Prasangika-Madhyamika. Also within the Svatantrika-Madhyamika again there is a division into two: the Yogachara-Svatantrika-Madhyamika School and the Sautrantika-Svatantrika-Madhyamika School. Both of these latter schools accept the sixth consciousness as the 'I' and this 'I' is identified as dependent on both the body and the mind. However, since the body ceases to exist at death, it is impossible simply to identify the 'I' in dependence on the body alone. Therefore, there is no alternative but to recognise consciousness itself as the 'I' according to this school of thought.

Now according to the Prasangika-Madhyamika School, all phenomena exist on the basis of interdependence. Similarly, 'I' exists on the basis of interdependence which is recognised as dependent on the combination of body and mind. 'I' therefore is a mere label on the combination of body and mind. Consciousness itself, alone, is not identified as the 'I'. The argument is that without investigation our natural feelings say that there is 'my body', 'my mind'. This we recognise and therefore it must be correct. Consequently 'my mind' is something belonging to 'I' and not 'I' itself (as is my body). So 'I' exists as a label on the combination of body and mind.

Now according to the Tantric tradition there are two 'I'. One temporary 'I', at the moment, as a human being, is a coarse or rough 'I' and this is labelled on the combination of the rough body and rough mind. At the same time there is a subtle 'I' and that is designated as dependent on the combination of the subtle body and subtle mind. In ordinary life this subtle body and subtle mind only appear inactive. At that time the subtle mind and body are manifest. So the 'I' that actually migrates to the next birth is the subtle 'I'.

Q. What is the nature of the subtle 'I'? What is the source of its qualities?
A. As before, its nature is a mere label on the subtle body (wind) and subtle mind. The subtle wind is itself seen as a body, but the subtle 'I' remains merely a label on the physical body.

Q. So the subtle wind has a manifest presence in the shape of my body?
A. Now, here 'wind' means some kind of energy, moving energy. So when we talk about the very subtle wind and the very subtle mind, the two are identified like this: the subtle mind on the basis of its being aware of an object and the subtle wind on the basis of an activation taking place towards a certain object. We are not really thinking about a physical body...the above two things combined we call the subtle 'I'. This is one entity with, you could say, two facets. The aspect which can reflect, or has the power of cognition, the quality of

awareness, is called the subtle mind. Simultaneously, there is its moving part, its energy, some kind of force which activates the mind towards the object. Now, this is—according to Buddhism—the real creator and this entity we also identify as Buddha-nature.

When that stage is realised, the stage beyond anger, beyond ordinary thought, at that level there is no longer the basis for the development of attachment, anger, jealousy, etc. All these qualities are secondary. This is the deepest level of the mind. For the present we cannot remain at that level. We move to a stage where there is a rougher mind and consequently the phenomenon of thought arises. But the ultimate Buddha-nature is entirely free from the qualities of the gross mind—and that mind itself remains full of awareness. That is the Buddha-mind.

Q. What, then, is the difference in quality between the peaceful forms of the deities and the wrathful forms of the deities?

A. Generally in Tantra two main paths are explained: one on the basis of taking attraction as the path and the other on the basis of taking aversion as the path. For both of these the aim is the same—the destruction of delusion.

Now there are different methods of eliminating delusion. For those who are not capable of using delusion as a path, to remove delusion itself, a path of separation from delusion has been taught. This is the way of the Hinayana teaching. Here the practitioner cannot himself utilise the poison (delusion)—so right from the beginning he always remains distant from it. The second method explained implies a dependence on delusion, through which one is able to free oneself from delusion and work for the benefit of others. In Bodhisattvayana, delusion is adopted in order to help other beings. In Sutrayana, under certain circumstances if it is helpful, delusion is relied upon. In Tantrayana the practitioner purposefully seeks the assistance of delusion—and not just from time to time.

Now the delusions themselves. There are three main types of delusion: ignorance, attraction (desire) and aversion (anger). Ignorance always acts as the basis of the other two. Therefore, the different methods of taking delusion as a path are of two types: one of taking desire and the other of taking anger as the path. Generally speaking, the deities concerned where anger is taken as the path are wrathful and where desire is taken as the path the deities are mainly peaceful. This is a broad way of classifying these two.

These two paths are also related to the individuals who are to practise them. Generally speaking, for those people who easily become angry the wrathful deity is more suitable; and for those people who are more influenced by desire or attachment the peaceful aspect is more suitable. Again, however, this is a general explanation.

Q. In conclusion, does Your Holiness have any general advice for practitioners in the West?

A. It is important to think very well before entering a particular spiritual tradition. Once you have entered one you should stick to it. Do not be like the man who tastes food in all the different restaurants but never actually gets down to eating a meal. Think carefully before adopting a practice; then follow it through. This way you will get some results from dedicating even a little time each day. Alternatively, if you try to follow all the various paths you will not get anywhere.

Also, patience in practice is required. In this age of machines everything seems to be automatic. You may think that it is the same with Dharma—that by merely turning on a switch you will gain realisation. Be patient. The development of mind takes time.

You should try to maintain a steady effort in practice. It is useless to try very hard for a few months, then give up this kind of application and then try very hard again. It is best to exert yourself in a constant and steady way. This is extremely important.

If you have adopted Buddhism you should not consider yourself a 'great Buddhist' and immediately start to do everything differently. A Tibetan proverb states, "Change your mind but leave your appearance as usual."

In all of Buddhism and especially in the Mahayana, the benefitting of others is heavily stressed. In this context Shantideva says in "Venturing into the Deeds of a Bodhisattva": "First investigate what is acceptable and what is unacceptable to the people (of the society in which you live); then avoid what is unacceptable." Of course, you must first consider whether or not what is acceptable and unacceptable is in contradiction to the Dharma. If the social norm does not contradict the Dharma you should try to live in accordance with it. In this way people will respect you. This is not done out of vanity but in order to bring the maximum benefit to all.

In Dharma practice it is necessary always to keep an attitude of love towards others, for this is the basis of bodhicitta. Love is a simple practice yet it is very beneficial for the individual who practises as well as for the community in which you live, for the nation and for the whole world. Love and kindness are always appropriate. Whether or not you believe in rebirth, you will need love in this life. If there is love, there is hope to have real families, real brotherhood, real equanimity, real peace. If the mind of love is lost, if you continue to see other beings as enemies, then no matter how much knowledge or education you have, no matter how much material progress is made, only suffering and confusion will ensue. Beings will continue to deceive and overpower one another. Basically, everyone exists in the very nature of suffering, so to abuse or mistreat each other is futile. The foundation of all spiritual practice is love. That you practise this well is my only request. Of course, to be able to do so in all situations will take time, but you should not lose courage. If you wish for happiness for mankind, love is the only way.

CHAPTER IV

Attitudes to Politics
and the Modern World

*Essays and discussions on social theories, the Tibetan political
situation, and aspects of the modern world*

Part One: Dharma and Politics

Happiness is man's prerogative. He seeks it and each man is equally entitled to his pursuit of happiness. No man seeks misery. Justice and equality belong to man's prerogatives too; but ones which should derive their practice from altruism and which have not been corroded by the stations of power and wealth. In order to build such an altruistic motivation so that justice and equality may co-exist in truth, the creation of a staunch moral fabric for the social environment is a prerequisite. Concerned voices are being raised about this inherent vacuum in the moral foundation of today since this lack is the foremost deterrent to a just and equal world.

The entire social structure must not only undergo a dynamic metamorphosis, but the chief constituent of this structure, the caretaker of society—man—must re-evaluate his attitudes, principles and values in order that such a change is seriously effected. The sceptics might question the possibility of altering the social system; but are we not the makers of our own environment? Man has created his social dilemmas, and if any change is to be forthcoming the power to do so lies with man alone.

Man and society are interdependent, hence the quality of man's behaviour as an individual and as a participant in his society is inseparable. Reparations have been attempted in the past as contributions to lessening the malaise and dysfunctional attitudes of our social world, in order to build a society which is more just and equal. Institutions and organisations have been established with their charters of noble ideology to combat these social problems. For all intents and purposes, the objectives have been laudable; but it has been unfortunate that basically good ideas have been defeated by man's inherent self-interest.

Today, ethics and moral principles sadly fall in the shadow of self-interest, particularly in the field of political culture. There is a school of thought which warns the moralist to refrain from politics as politics is devoid of ethics and moral principles. This is a wrong approach since politics devoid of ethics does not further the benefits to man and his society, and life without morality will make men no better than beasts. The political concept is not axiomatically 'dirty', a common adjective ascribed to politics today: but the instruments of our political culture have tampered with and distorted the fundamental concepts of fine ideals to further their own selfish ends. Today, spiritual people are voicing their concern about the intermingling of politics with religion since they fear the violation of ethics by politics which, according to them, would thereby contaminate the purity of religion. This line of thought is both selfish and contradictory. All religions exist to serve and help man and any divorce from politics is to forsake a powerful instrument for social welfare. Religion and politics is a useful combination for the welfare of mankind, when tempered by correct ethical concepts with a minimum of self-interest.

In the correlation between ethics and politics, should deep moral convictions form the guideline for the political practitioner, man and his society will reap far-reaching benefits. It is an absurd assumption that religion and morality have no place in politics and that a man of religion and a believer in morality should seclude himself as a hermit. These ideas lack proper perspective vis-a-vis man's relation to his society and the role of politics in our lives. Strong moral ethics are as concomitantly crucial to a man of politics as they are to a man of religion, for dangerous consequences are foreseen when our politicians and those who rule forget their moral principles and convictions. Irrespective of whether we are a believer or an agnostic, whether we believe in God or karma, moral ethics is a code which everyone is able to pursue. We need human qualities such as moral scruples, compassion and humility. In recognition of human frailty and weakness, these qualities are only accessible through forceful individual development in a conducive social milieu, so that a more humane world will come into being as an ultimate goal. Self-realisation that materialism does not foster the growth of morals, compassion and humility should be innately created. The functional importance of religious and social institutions towards promoting these qualities thus assumes a serious responsibility and all efforts should be concentrated sincerely in fulfilling these needs. Prejudice and bias should be forgotten and different religions should work in unity not only for the creation of these qualities in man, but also for an atmosphere of harmony and understanding. The world has become communicably smaller today and, with respect to its limitations, no nation can survive in isolation. It is in our own interest to create a world of love, justice and equality, for without a sense of universal responsibility based on morality, our existence and survival is at a perilous precipice.

The qualities required to create such a world must be inculcated right from the beginning, when the child is young. We cannot expect our generation or the new generation to make the change without this basic foundation. If there is any hope it is in the future generation, but not unless we initiate a major change in our present educational system on a world-wide basis.

A dynamic revolution is deemed crucial for instigating a political culture founded on moral ethics. Such a revolution must be sponsored by the powerful nations, for any such attempt by the smaller and the weaker nations is unlikely to succeed. If powerful nations adopt policies based on a bed-rock of moral principles and if they concern themselves genuinely with the welfare of mankind, a new path and a new ray of hope will emerge. Such a revolution will surpass all other attempts to achieve justice and equality in our world.

I feel very strongly about this subject of moral ethics and appeal to all humanists and those who share my concern to contribute to making our society and our world more compassionate, more just and more equitable.

Part Two: Justice and the Society

(A talk to the Wayne State students of law)

A human society without laws aimed at establishing justice will find itself enmeshed in suffering. The strong will impose their will upon the weak, the wealthy upon the poor, the governing upon the governed. So justice is something very important within society. If we lose sight of it we ourselves will greatly suffer as a result.

Many of you in the audience are students of law. I think that your work will not be easy. At the moment the world atmosphere is not very just, both for individual nations and within the international community. But we Tibetans have a saying: "If nine efforts fail, try a tenth." It makes me happy to speak with people seriously attempting to create a just world. If you really work for justice you will meet with much failure, much disappointment; yet this effort is still very important.

I am told that you have some interest to hear something about our political situation. Since my visit to this country (U.S.A., 1979) is mainly religious, educational, social and non-political in nature, it is difficult for me to speak on politics. But then, sometimes one creates a dynamic impression by saying something, and sometimes creates as significant an impression by remaining silent. I think it is more useful here to remain silent. At the moment the Asian political situation is changing rapidly, and many things that now appear static in actual fact are not as secure as is believed. My own view is to do what I can and to wait patiently, watching the situation. Who knows what may happen?

Most of you here are interested in law. Law, education, science, technology, politics, religion: all these things are meant to be means for benefitting the society and living beings. Benefit here means to bring joy to them, to increase their happiness. There are both material and spiritual means to accomplish this end, but both aim at the same thing: happiness.

All human beings, despite cultural, social, political and racial differences, are essentially the same in that they all have an innate grasping at 'I' and, based on that grasping, an instinctive wish for happiness. All the millions of humans on this planet are concerned primarily and on an instinctive level with the wish for happiness. This has been their main concern throughout the past, and will be so in the future.

106

Because of this truth I have no difficulty to sit before you here and speak with you. I come from Tibet far beyond the Himalayan mountains and you are students of law here in America; yet because of the presence of this basic human element in both of us I feel a sameness with you, like sitting with an old friend. Although we are meeting physically today for the first time, I sense a human brotherhood between us. On that basis it is possible to share a closeness. If we can really feel that closeness, then working together for a just and harmonious society becomes natural.

At present the world is suffering from great conflicts, such as those in the Middle-East, South-East Asia and so forth, on top of the general East-West confrontation problem. All of these arise from a lack of understanding of one another's human-ness. The answer to them is not an armaments race or a show of force, but an understanding of the common human quality that I spoke about above. The solution is not technological or political, it is spiritual; a sensitive understanding of our common situation. Hatred and fighting cannot bring happiness to anyone, even to the perpetrator of these acts. Prosperity is born from social harmony. Destruction and violence always produce misery. It is time for the world to learn to transcend differences of race, culture and ideology, and to regard one another through eyes which understand the common human situation.

This would benefit the individual, the community and the nation. As all nations are now dependent upon one another economically, this human understanding must exceed the bounds of the nation and embrace the international community. If peoples everywhere are not allowed to strive for the happiness they instinctively want, then they will be dissatisfied and will make problems for everyone. Unless we can create an atmosphere of genuine co-operation—a co-operation not gained by threat of force but by heartfelt understanding—life will become ever more difficult. If we can satisfy people at a heart-level, peace will ensue. Without this basis of co-existence, if undesirable social, political and cultural forms continue to be imposed upon people, peace becomes difficult. Within the nation each individual must be made happy, and between nations there must be equal concern for the wishes of the smallest. I am not saying here that one system today is better than others and that all should adopt that one; on the contrary, a variety of systems and ideologies is desirable as there is a variety of dispositions within the human community. This variety could enhance the collective happiness of mankind. Each national community should be free to evolve its own political and social system. But the basis of them all must be self-determination, both on an individual and a national level.

Part Three: Realities and Misconceptions of the Tibetan Issue

Recently (Summer, 1976) a flood of articles on Tibet has appeared in the *New York Times* and many other newspapers throughout the world. Many of these articles contained patently false information about the situation in Tibet and the position of the Tibetans in exile. I feel, therefore, that it is time I myself contributed a brief article towards clearing up some of these misconceptions.

Tibet is geographically, racially and culturally different from China. Historically, too, Tibet has always been an independent country, and has never been 'an integral part of China'. The very fact that it now has to be referred to as 'part of China' is a clear indication of its separate, independent status in the past. If it had always been a part of China, what was the need of changing the boundaries on the maps of Central Asia prepared after 1959?

Another indication of Tibet's independent status is the great pains taken by the Chinese communists to explain to the Tibetans the status of Tibet. They make a distinction between China and the 'Middle Kingdom'. They have been stressing to us that Tibet isn't part of China, but that it is under the Middle Kingdom just as is China. Tibet and China, they explain, enjoy equal status and both are parts of the Middle Kingdom.

After the signing of the '17-point Agreement' when the first Tibetan delegation, headed by Kalon T.T. Liushar, called on Mao Tse-Tung, the latter told Kalon Liushar: "Now that Tibet has returned to the motherland, Peking is your city, Shanghai is your city." To this Kalon Lukhangwa, my then Prime Minister, later remarked in Lhasa: "We do not want Peking or Shanghai, give us back Chamdo." Chamdo, third largest city in Tibet, was kept under military administration by the Chinese from the time of their invasion until the establishment of the Preparatory Committee for the Autonomous Region of Tibet.

In official documents, Tibetans now enjoy the same rights as the Chinese, but when it comes to implementation the Tibetans are treated as second-class citizens in their own country. Tibetans have been forcibly recruited into labour gangs to construct roads, military installations and buildings. Hundreds of schools have also been built, but refugees who still manage to trickle out maintain that these cannot be called Tibetan schools as only a little Tibetan is taught in the beginning grades. The rest of the curriculum consists of Chinese language and history, basic arithmetic and manual labour. The thousands of kilometres of roads constructed since the Chinese takeover aren't of much use to the Tibetans since there isn't any public transportation.

Improvement has also been made in agricultural output but, according to refugees, at the time of the harvest most of the grain is taken away by the Chinese as 'Surplus Grain Sale', 'State Grain Tax', 'Commune Development Tax', 'War Preparation Grain' etc., and the Tibetans are left with a meagre ration of between 90 to 120 kilogrammes of barley per person per year.

It is for these reasons that the Tibetan communists, who had been most enthusiastic in the beginning, not only started to become disillusioned by about 1956 but eventually many of them openly resented the Chinese actions in Tibet. The result was that most of the Tibetan communists were dismissed from their official posts and quietly deported to China.

We admit that the social and governmental system of the past in Tibet was neither faultless nor suited to the changing times. But Tibetans were prepared to change of their own accord. Even before 1959 I brought about some reforms, but the Chinese weren't happy when we started to do these on our own. They didn't give their blessings. They wanted to reap the maximum benefit out of the reforms that they were planning to carry out, and our action was endangering this prospect. Tibetans in exile still are for gradual modernity and change. With these aspirations in mind, I promulgated in 1963 the draft of a constitution for a future Tibet. I also said in an official statement a few years ago that the rule of the Dalai Lama may or may not continue in future Tibet, and that we might even adopt socialistic systems. We are, therefore, not against change or reform.

There isn't any doubt that China has made tremendous progress since the communist takeover. The masses have also benefitted from this. I admit that even in Tibet they have brought about many changes which were necessary but which might not have been possible for us to carry out. But at what cost and sacrifice have they achieved this? In terms of human lives and freedom, that we cherish so sacredly, the sacrifices have been tremendous and terrible, to say the least.

What has happened very often is this: in order to meet certain targets and to please higher authorities, Chinese officials have adopted every means, fair or foul, and completely failed to take into account the sufferings and feelings of the people, who in most cases have to pretend that they are happy even when they are not.

And the most unfortunate part of this whole process has been that the high officials were quite oblivious to what had actually happened on the spot, and accepted unquestioningly the reports of their subordinates, even when they contained absolutely untrue statements. For example, while a certain section of the population might have strongly resented the impiementation of a project, the report might say that the people wholeheartedly joined the PLA and the party in its implementation.

About 50,000 Tibetans including myself, who left the country in 1959, had already experienced nine years of Chinese rule in Tibet. All those years I tried to reach an amicable solution with them because the inc itable result otherwise would have been an open clash between the Tibetan people and the Chinese troops, in which case the former would unquestionably be in a disadvantageous position. Unfortunately, the situation deteriorated so fast that all my efforts were in vain and the open clash did take place in March 1959, with predictable results.

The tragedy of Tibet is that a whole race, a people strongly opposed to foreign domination, has been subjugated, oppressed and devoured by China. This has happened not only to Tibet, but also to Mongolia and Eastern Turkestan (Sinkiang). It may not sound right for me to speak of these two other countries, which are in a similar situation, but I happen to know the true feelings and the national aspirations of these people. Their feelings of resentment against Chinese domination are no less than those of the Tibetans.

To make it easier to devour the invaded nations, the Chinese try to cut them into pieces. They persist, for example, in dividing Tibet into two parts: Inne: and Outer Tibet Historical facts and existing realities mean nothing to them. In all their propaganda, they only mean Outer Tibet when they say 'Tibet' or more officially, 'The Autonomous Region of Tibet'. This means the cutting away of about half of Tibet's territory, and about two-thirds of our population. In this part of Tibe. —the Inner Tibet—we have the Amdo and the Kham provinces which traditionally were inseparable from the rest of Tibet. No Tibetan or learned scholar on Tibet can imagine Tibet or Tibetans without the Amdo and the Kham provinces. The whole of Tibet, without this mythical distinction, has suffered under the invasion by communist China and has been determined in its struggle against the unjust foreign domination.

In fact it was in the eastern part of Tibet, which the Chinese call Inner Tibet, that the initial sporadic revolts against the Chinese occupation took place, so much so that the Tibetan resistance movement has often been mislabelled as a Khampa resistance movement.

Even today, there are recent reports that desperate acts of fighting and sabotage have been carried out in these regions. Another clear indication of continued Tibetan resistance and failure on the part of the communist Chinese to win over the Tibetans completely is the lack of any prominent Tibetan from among the younger generation to toe their line—a generation that the Chinese has had ample time to groom and indoctrinate since 1950.

It is well-known that the Chinese have made a similar arbitrary demarcation in the case of Mongolia as well.

The struggle to free ourselves was and is a Tibetan initiative and a Tibetan movement. In the process of our struggle we have welcomed external help whenever it didn't go against our basic goal, and have shunned it whenever it did. But because our struggle is just and we believe in it, it could not and cannot be abandoned even if no help were to come at all.

Some parties persist in calling the Tibetans in exile 'a handful of reactionary cliques'. (Some have given the figure 15,000.) To me this need never be a subject of controversy. India and all other countries where there are Tibetan refugees are open societies. The truth or falsehood of claims by 'about 100,000 refugees' can easily be verified by visiting these places.

The world has seen how unpredictable and inconsistent the Chinese are through the vicissitudes in the lives of Liu Shao-chi, Lin Piao, Teng Hsiao-ping and, more recently, the 'Gang of Four'. These acts are unprincipled and conducted at the whim of a few individuals. One can imagine how much the Tibetans have also suffered through such vicissitudes under the Chinese rule.

The Chinese have recently extended an 'invitation' to the Tibetans in exile, including myself, to return home. When the offer became known a number of newspapers hinted that it might be 'profitable' for me to return now. Some even informed their readers that some sort of secret and indirect negotiation was going on between my representatives and the Chinese leaders.

These rumours confirm that people in the West have totally misunderstood the true nature of our struggle. The issue isn't whether the Dalai

Lama and the 100,000 refugees would be able to return to Tibet. The reason we appeal to other nations isn't because we want to go back and the Chinese aren't allowing us in. It isn't that I long for some of the privileges I used to enjoy and am bitter with the Chinese for having reduced me to the status of a refugee. The Chinese have been asking us to return since the end of 1963. Most of their offers have been regularly broadcast on Radio Lhasa and through printed leaflets. There has been no response from our side on this issue. The real issues are the feelings and welfare of the six million Tibetans still left in Tibet. Why should an alien rule be forced upon them? Why shouldn't they have the choice of holding their own beliefs, traditions, culture and identity?

If those six million Tibetans there are really happy and contented we would be prepared to return and accept whatever status the majority of them are prepared to grant us. But first it should be established to the total satisfaction of all the Tibetans in exile that the Tibetans in Tibet are completely satisfied with their lot. This is the only prerequisite. There isn't any question of 'secret negotiations' to make it possible for me to return.

So far, what the Chinese have claimed either directly or through a few selected visitors hasn't succeeded in convincing us. Some of these visitors have always been uncritical admirers of the 'Chinese Revolution'. They make their living out of reporting first-hand news from China and commenting on it. How can they be expected to say anything that would conceivably jeopardise their chances of obtaining more Chinese visas in future? Fortunately, some recent visitors have tried to give an objective account of their visits to Tibet and I hope there are more and more such visitors in future.

In spite of many difficulties, we have been getting information about the conditions inside Tibet. We consider this to be of utmost importance, because we must act according to the wishes of the majority of our people.

In short, what is needed is what I have constantly been demanding: an internationally supervised plebiscite, both inside and outside Tibet, to determine whether the Tibetans in Tibet are happy. The plebiscite should be conducted throughout Tibet and it should also include in its investigative body people who can understand and speak Tibetan, so that they don't need to depend solely on Chinese interpreters. It might even include one or two Tibetans, who don't have to be selected or recommended by me. I am prepared to accept whatever verdicts and recommendations such a plebiscite discovers.

Part Four: China and the Future of Tibet

During the past few weeks (Sept.'79) I have visited many parts of the United States and spoken at universities, colleges and religious institutions and at small centres of learning. I have also had the opportunity to address several organisations concerned with world affairs and foreign policy. In almost every situation I have taken the liberty to speak on love and compassion. I firmly believe that the promotion of these qualities can contribute to modern society's need for a balance against excessive material preoccupation.

I have spoken at length on these topics not simply as a Buddhist, but from a clear universal recognition that except for superficial differences all humans are in essence the same in that we all want happiness and do not want suffering, and on this basis engage in various techniques to bring this about. Recognition of our fundamental aim and agreement is important.

The press, the general public and numerous individuals I have met have also indicated a keen interest in Tibet, the Tibetan people and their future. It is obvious that developments in China during the past few years have contributed to this interest and caused speculations of a quick end to my exile.

Therefore I think that I should express my thoughts on the subject and my views on what may possibly lie ahead.

One who is not politically prejudiced can easily understand that Tibet is a separate country, different from China. This thought comes quite naturally because Tibet was and is in fact different from China—racially, culturally, linguistically, geographically and historically. No knowledgeable person would for a moment think that Tibetans are Chinese.

In the past there existed a special patron-priest relationship between China and Tibet, a relationship which was spiritual rather than temporal. In those times, the three countries—China, Mongolia and Tibet—were referred to as separate countries. You ask a Tibetan what his nationality is and his answer will be 'Tibetan'. Similarly, when people discuss something Tibetan, it is always in the sense of something that is different and distinct from Japanese, Indian or Chinese. For example, when people talk about Tibetan Buddhism, it is never implied that Chinese Buddhism represents Tibetan Buddhism as well.

The word 'China' is 'Gya-nak' in Tibetan. Since the Tibetan word 'Gya-nak' refers to a foreign land, it implies Tibet to be separate from China. The Chinese do not use this word. They use the vague terms 'our nation' and 'motherland' instead of 'China' in their official documents and publications in the Tibetan language. They explain to us that Tibet is not a part of Gya-nak (China), but that it is a part of Chung Kuo (Middle Kingdom), just as Gya-nak (China) also is! However, Chinese who are not politically oriented do not make this distinction, for they refer to the Chinese language as Chung Kuo Hua (language of the Middle Kingdom). But politically motivated Chinese refer to it as Han Hua (language of Han) in order to justify their stand that Tibet is an integral part of the Middle Kingdom. Linguistic concoctions cannot hide the facts of life and history.

Because Tibet as well as Mongolia and East Turkestan are basically and historically different from China, the Chinese have established various autonomous administrative systems in these occupied areas. They also use the language of these countries along with Chinese on their currency notes. Also, in the case of Tibet, because it was independent until 1950, the Chinese signed the 17-point Agreement with the Tibetan Government. No other Chinese-occupied nationality has any such agreement, pact or treaty with China. Here again, the Chinese say that this is an 'agreement' and not a 'treaty', giving the unsatisfactory explanation that 'agreements' are made only within a nation between the central and local governments.

It may be of interest that Sun Yat-sen, the father of the Chinese Republic, considered Tibet, Mongolia and Manchuria as foreign countries. Also, Mao Tse-tung, in the 1930s when he was carrying out his struggle and was not yet in power, supported Tibetan independence. Many years later, in 1954 when I was in China, Mao told me that while we were poor and backward, China would help us, but that after 20 years we (Tibetans) would be able to help them (the Chinese). On another occasion he told me that the Chinese personnel then stationed in Tibet would be withdrawn when the Tibetans could manage by themselves.

Even after 30 years of occupation by the People's Republic of China—and in spite of China's world-wide propaganda projecting the picture of Tibet as an inseparable and integral part of China — nobody says that he has been to 'China' when he has visited 'Tibet', or that the 'Chinese' have taken to socialism when he means that the 'Tibetans' have.

During these past three decades the Chinese have placed great emphasis on the unity of their nation and have boasted much achievement in that direction. Speeches on this have been made on numerous occasions at public meetings and official receptions. If we are to go by the number of times this theme has been stressed, by now the Chinese should have achieved a rock-like unshakable unity. But this has not happened, for it is an artificial unity that is being imposed unsuccessfully on different nationalities, Tibetans being one of them.

To claim that Tibet is a part of the Chinese nation is both distorted and hypocritical. The Chinese seem to realise this, and one hopes therefore that they will change their policy and accept the reality of a Tibetan nation. If the Chinese really want understanding and friendship, Tibetans, Mongolians and East Turkestanis should be treated according to their real circumstances and should be given their inalienable national rights and fundamental freedoms in their own homelands.

The Chinese claim that they did not come to Tibet as imperialists or colonialists, but as 'liberators'. What sort of liberation is it that denies the people their birthright and the freedom to determine their own destiny themselves? Having deprived the Tibetan people of freedom, the Chinese talk about an imaginary 'state of glorious happiness and progress' said to be existing in Tibet.

I am pointing out these facts not with any antagonism toward the Chinese. If one day all the countries of the world join together as one nation, I would welcome that, and Tibet would become a willing partner in such a movement. But as long as this does not happen, the six million Tibetans are entitled to all the rights that other free peoples have, including the preservation of their separate, unique identity and way of life. As long as the six million Tibetans remain under foreign military occupation, they will continue to struggle for genuine national liberation and for legitimate rights in their own country.

I think it is important that we Tibetans present a clear and factual account of the Tibetan situation. This is particularly necessary now when the present Chinese leadership is reported to be following a more moderate and reasonable path. It remains to be seen whether Chinese leaders are prepared to recognise realities as they really exist, or whether they will continue to direct facts in order to draw conclusions that serve only China's interests.

I have always firmly believed that unless we act according to the real existing circumstances we can never achieve our true aspirations. To my great disappointment, ever since the invasion of Tibet by the People's Republic of China, owing both to a lack of understanding of the actual situation, and often because the truth was intentionally ignored by the Chinese, there have existed most unfriendly relations between Tibet and China. This is an unfortunate state of affairs between two countries who have been neighbours for centuries. The Chinese took advantage of the Tibetans whenever possible, and as a result the Tibetans have grown ever suspicious of them.

Unions or federations can take place only when there is mutual agreement and mutual benefits flow from such arrangements. But they have to be disbanded or discontinued when it is realised that the people do not support them. The future of Tibet is not a matter of determination by the Chinese occupation force. Six million Tibetans obviously cannot be absorbed or integrated into China and their identity cannot be destroyed.

Friendly relations between Tibet and China, which I dearly wish for, can be established only on the basis of equality, mutual respect and mutual benefit. I for one would gladly accept whatever destiny the six million people of Tibet choose for themselves in a climate of genuine freedom and peace. The free will of the Tibetan people is the only true basis for determining their destiny. Until it flourishes, there will be no peace in the hearts and minds of my people. With boundless faith in themselves and in the righteousness of their own cause they will wait for the day, which must come, when they can fully and freely enjoy their legitimate national rights and at the same time enjoy a relationship with China on a new basis of mutual benefit and respect.

Part Five: Spiritual Contributions to Social Progress

Material progress alone is not sufficient to achieve an ideal society. Even in countries where great external progress has been made, mental problems have increased, causing additional hardships. No amount of legislation or coercion can accomplish the well-being of society, for this depends upon the internal attitude of the people who comprise it.

Therefore, mental development, in company and in harmony with material development, is very important. Since the development of a healthy social attitude built around a sense of consideration and kindness for others is vital to society, the cultivation of kindness, love and compassion cannot be limited, as has often been the case, to religious believers. Rather, whether one is a believer or not, the value of kindness and consideration is appreciated by all and therefore should be cultivated by everyone.

Anger and hatred cannot bring harmony. The noble task of arms control and disarmament cannot be accomplished by confrontation and condemnation. Hostile attitudes only serve to heat up the situation, whereas a true sense of respect gradually cools down what otherwise could become explosive. We must recognise the frequent contradiction between short-term benefit and long-term harm.

Regardless of race, creed, ideology, political bloc (East and West) or economic region (North and South), the most important and basic aspect of all peoples is their shared humanity—the fact that each person, old, young, rich, poor, educated, uneducated, male or female, is a human. This shared human-ness and thus the shared aspiration of gaining happiness and avoiding suffering, as well as the basic right to bring these about, are of prime importance.

All of the means to bring these about—economic and political systems, ideologies, religious creeds and so forth—are secondary. These should be utilised for the main purpose, and not allowed to become primary and thereby obstacles to achieving what should be primary—the well-being of society.

The various spiritual systems basically have the same message of making better human beings. Though they espouse different philosophies, we should not concentrate on these differences to the extent of losing sight of the common aim and result—improving human beings. From this point of view, the adherents to the many different religious systems should develop mutual respect. Each system has its own value suited to persons of different disposition and mental outlook. At this time of easy communication, we must increase our efforts to learn each other's systems. This does not mean that we should make all religions into one but that we should recognise the common purpose of the many religions and value the different techniques that they have developed for internal improvement.

The benefits gained through internal improvement are not limited to religious practitioners. Both believers and non-believers gain from development of these attitudes fundamental to society. Still, even if believers and non-believers have this commonality, are Buddhism and communism, for instance, not basically at odds with each other? It is a reality of today's world that much of Buddhist civilisation, stretching from the borders of Thailand to parts of Siberia, is under the sway of communist ideology. This area is inhabited by more than a quarter of mankind, the vast majority of whom are Buddhists.

Communism has not, however, been able to eradicate people's faith in Buddhism. It may seem shocking, but when one considers the experience of the past few decades and the trend of the foreseeable future, it may be wise to attempt a dialogue between communism and Buddhism. Millions of people have suffered due to the estrangement of these two systems. When the Buddhists view the communists with suspicion and distrust and vice versa, the two only become more estranged and the possibility of either one effectively helping the people in this region lessens.

Theoretically, original Marxism and Mahayana Buddhism, despite many differences, also have many basic points in common. The foremost is the emphasis on the common good of society. Therefore, the adherents of these two systems could develop respect for each other.

Also, among religions, Buddhism is atheistic in the sense that a creator god is not accepted; rather, Buddhism presents a view of self-creation, that one's own actions create one's life situation. In this light, it has been said that Buddhism is not a religion, but a science of the mind.

In Buddhism, it is explained that everything depends on one's own karma. This means that one's life situation in the present depends upon one's actions and their motivations in the past and that one's future is thus capable of being moulded through engaging in salutary actions with a pure motivation. Similarly, in communist or Marxist theory everything is said to depend on one's own labour.

Furthermore, Marxist economic theory is related with ethical principles in the sense that the prime concern is with the use of resources and wealth, not their mere accumulation. The emphasis is not on the accumulation of money but the proper use of it for the welfare of the needy majority. Likewise, in Buddhism the practice of considering the needs of other beings is stressed to such an extent that one sacrifices the welfare of the minority and oneself, for the benefit of the majority of sentient beings. All practice is seen as a means for serving others.

The original thrust of communism was toward anti-exploitation and anti-corruption; it was not necessarily anti-religion. Some religious institutions had come to involve corruption; thus they had to be opposed. Likewise, although Marxism has good points, the implementations of some of its practices are corrupt and therefore have to be opposed. In this way, a distinction must be made between systems and their practitioners.

In general, all religions are anti-exploitation and against social injustice. Buddha himself, in a revolutionary way, overcame rigid class boundaries, explaining a system of inner mental development that is open to persons from all walks of life.

Since the thrust of Marxist thought is not absolutely anti-religion, there is no point in religious people viewing Marxism as anti-religious, creating tension and distrust. The commonality of many aims should and must be stressed. Similarly, Marxists, out of ignorance and lack of personal experience, see religion as totally counterproductive, which is wrong. A real Marxist must discard narrow and dogmatic attitudes, and be open to the value of spiritual teachings.

The reason for developing such an attitude is not the preservation of religion but successful improvement of society. The experience of the last few decades yields sufficient evidence that the Marxist ideology is not a full answer for human society—it has its good and bad points.

If it were adequate for the development of human society, there would be no need for contribution from other systems. However, it seems that some of its followers have destroyed one privileged social class only to create another in its place. Mental and creative developments have stagnated and brought fear and mistrust in society. This shows the need for the inner, moral development of a socially oriented attitude.

History has shown that no single political, economic or social ideology has been sufficient. So it seems worthwhile for the two great systems

119

of this large expanse of the world to take points from each other. Certainly, Buddhist theory is not sufficient by itself for a full socio-economic policy in this or the next century; it can take many points from Marxist, socialist and democratic systems. Similarly, those systems can benefit from many points in Buddhist theory, especially in terms of the development of socially beneficial attitudes. Such a partnership would help millions of people.

For the development of a peaceful, friendly human family of nations with a rich variety of faiths and political and economic systems, each of us has the responsibility to strive towards such harmony. There is no alternative.

Part Six: Meeting-Points Of Science and Spirituality

I have always believed that the ultimate aim of humanity is genuine happiness and satisfaction. That is what I believe and what I take as the basic starting-point. In order to achieve the maximum happiness and satisfaction, we need to understand everything that is connected with mankind and his quest for happiness, whether it be in the field of matter or in the spiritual field. Then, taking advantage of our knowledge of the different approaches, we have to find the right method to follow in order to achieve that aim.

The knowledge of external phenomena, and the application of that knowledge, is that which nowadays we call science. The approach and methods which focus primarily on internal phenomena—consciousness or the mind—constitute another sphere of knowledge. Both have the same objective, the achievement of happiness and satisfaction, which are the intimate concern of every human being. Not only the objective, but the method is also directly related to human beings as it is the individual person who puts it into action. The scientist investigating external phenomena is still a living human being who wants happiness; whether it is his profession or not, consciousness is also his concern. The spiritual person, whose interest lies in consciousness, or meditation, has to deal with matter. No one single way is sufficient; indeed if just one approach had been found to be so, the need would never have been felt to bring these disciplines together.

Both approaches are therefore very important, and I should like to say a few words to relate them to one another.

The fundamental view or philosophy of Buddhism is that of 'dependent arising'. When one talks about the view of dependent arising one means that things exist in dependence or that they are imputed depending on something or other. In the case of a physical phenomenon, one would specify that it exists in dependence on its parts, whereas non-physical composite phenomena would be described as existing in dependence either on their continuity or an aspect of their continuity. Consequently, whether it be external or internal phenomena there is not anything that exists except in dependence upon its parts or aspects.

If one were to investigate to find a basis for the imputation in any given phenomenon, since one would not find anything at all which actually is the phenomenon—no solid lump of anything that one could point one's finger at, which represents the phenomenon—then one says that phenomena exist through the imputation of the mind.

As phenomena do not exist independently of the imputing mind, one speaks of 'emptiness', which means the lack of any intrinsic existence that does not depend upon the imputing mind. Since things do not exist just of their own accord, but in dependence on conditions, they change whenever they encounter different conditions. Thus, they come into existence in dependence on conditions and they cease in dependence on conditions. That very lack of any intrinsic existence, independent of cause and conditions, is the basis for all the changes that are possible in a phenomenon, such as birth, cessation and so forth.

It may be interesting to compare the scientific interpretation of the role of the observer or 'participator' with the Buddhist view that observed phenomena do not exist merely as a mental image, a projection or vision of the mind, but rather that they exist as separate entities from the mind. Mind and matter are two separate things. Matter is separate from the mind which cognises it and denominates it. This means that, with regard to all phenomena without exception, though they are not simply a creation or manifestation of the mind having no entity of their own, yet their ultimate mode of existence is dependent on the mind that imputes them—the 'imputer'. Their mode of existence is therefore quite separate from the imputer, but their existence itself is dependent on the imputer. I feel that this point of view perhaps corresponds to the scientific explanation of the role of the observer. Although different terms are employed to explain them, their meanings are somewhat related.

On the surface, the dependent arising and emptiness explained above may seem to be quite contradictory. Yet if one analyses them on a much deeper level, one can come to understand that phenomena, on account of their being empty, are dependently arising or dependently existing, and because of that dependent existence, they are empty by nature. Thus one can establish both emptiness and dependent arising on one single basis, and thereby two faces which, on a general level, seem to be contradictory, when understood on a very profound level, will be seen to fit together in a very complementary fashion.

The mode of existence of phenomena is differentiated from their mode of appearance. Phenomena appear to the mind differently from their actual mode of existence. When the mind apprehends their way of appearing, believes in that appearance as being true, and follows that particular idea or concept, then one makes mistakes. Since that concept is completely distorted in its apprehension of the objects, it contradicts the actual mode of existence, or reality itself. So this disparity or contradiction between 'what is' and 'what appears' is due to the fact that although phenomena are in reality empty of any intrinsic nature, yet they do appear to the ordinary mind as if they exist inherently, although they lack any such quality. Similarly, although in reality things which depend on causes are impermanent and transient, undergoing constant change, they do appear as though they were permanent and unchanging. Again, something that in its true nature is suffering appears as happiness. And something which is in reality false appears as true. There are many levels of subtlety regarding this contradiction between the mode of existence of phenomena and their mode of appearance. As a result of the contradiction between 'what is' and 'what appears', there arise all manner of mistakes. This explanation may have much in common with scientists' views of the difference in the modes of appearance and existence of certain phenomena.

Generally speaking, an understanding of the meaning of emptiness and dependent arising will naturally lead one to a deeper conviction in the law of cause and effect, where, as a result of different causes and conditions, corresponding fruits or effects, positive or negative, arise. One will then pay more attention to the causes and also be more aware of the various conditions. If one has a good understanding of emptiness or familiarity with it, then the arising of distortions, like attachment, hatred and so on, in the mind will diminish, since they are caused by a mistaken view—mistaken in not correctly distinguishing between 'what is' and 'what appears'. One can see, for instance, from one's own experience how one's feeling towards something that one observes will change, depending on one's own state of mind. Although the object remains the same, one's reaction will be far less intense when one's mind is calm than if it is overcome by some strong emotional feeling, like anger. The actual mode of existence of phenomena, the bare truth of existence, is emptiness. When one understands this, and appreciates the contradictory nature of the appearance of phenomena, one will immediately be able to realise this mistaken view to be untrue. Consequently all of the mental distortions such as attachment, hatred, etc., which are based on that misconception, a deception rooted in the contradictory nature of phenomena, will decrease in strength.

We might ask: how do the different levels of the consciousness or mind that apprehends an object actually come to exist themselves? Different levels of consciousness established are in relation to the different levels of subtlety of the inner energy that activates and moves the consciousness towards a given object. So, the level of their subtlety and strength in moving the consciousness towards the object determines and establishes the different levels of consciousness. It is very important to reflect upon the relationship between the inner consciousness and outer material substances. Many Eastern philosophies, and in particular Buddhism, speak of four elements: earth, water, fire and air, or five elements with the addition of space. The first four elements, earth, water, fire and air are supported by the element of space, which enables them to exist and to function. Space or 'ether' serves, then, as the basis for the functioning of all the other elements.

These five elements can be divided into two types: the outer five elements and the inner five elements, and there is a definite relationship between the outer and inner elements. As regards the element of space or 'ether', according to certain Buddhist texts such as the Kalachakra Tantra space is not just a total voidness, devoid of anything at all, but is referred to in terms of 'empty particles'. This empty particle therefore serves as the basis for the evolution and dissolution of the four other elements. They are generated from it and finally are absorbed back into it. The process of dissolution evolves in the order: earth, water, fire and air, and the process of generation in the order: air, fire, water and earth. These four are better understood in terms of solidity (earth), liquids (water), heat (fire) and energy (air). The four elements are generated from the subtle level to the gross, out of this basis of empty particles, and they dissolve from the gross level to the subtle into the empty particles. Space, or the empty particle, is the basis for the whole process.

The 'Big Bang' model of the beginning of the universe has perhaps something in common with this empty particle. Also, the most subtle, fine particle described in modern physics seems to be similar to the empty particle. Such parallels do present something that I feel it would be worthwhile to reflect upon.

From the spiritual point of view of Buddhism, the state of our mind, whether it is disciplined or undisciplined, produces what is known as 'karma'. This is accepted in many Eastern philosophies. Karma, meaning 'action', has a particular influence upon the inner elements, which in turn affect the outer elements. This, too, is a point for further investigation.

Another area in Tibetan Buddhism which may be of interest to scientists is the relationship between the physical elements and the nerves, and consciousness, in particular the relationship between the elements in the brain and consciousness. Involved here are the changes in consciousness, happy or unhappy states of mind etc., the kind of effect they have on the elements within the brain, and the consequent effect that has on the body. Certain physical illnesses improve or worsen according to the state of mind. Regarding this kind of relationship between body and mind, Buddhism can definitely make a contribution to modern science.

Buddhism also explains, with great precision, the different levels of subtlety within consciousness itself. These are very clearly described in the Tantra, and research on these, in my opinion, would produce very beneficial results. Consciousness is classified, from the point of view of its level of subtlety, into three levels: the waking state or gross level of consciousness, the consciousness of the dream state, which is more subtle, and the consciousness during deep dreamless sleep, which is subtler still.

Similarly, the three stages of birth, death and the intermediate state are also established in terms of the subtlety of their levels of consciousness. During the process of dying, a person experiences the innermost, subtle consciousness; the consciousness becomes grosser after death in the intermediate state, and progressively more gross during the process of birth. Upon the basis of the continuity of the stream of consciousness is established the existence of rebirth and reincarnation. There are currently a number of well-documented cases of individuals who clearly remember their past lives, and it would seem that it would be very worthwhile to investigate these phenomena, with a view to expanding human knowledge.

Part Seven: Questions and Answers

1. THE FUTURE FOR TIBET

Q. In an interview that Your Holiness gave some years ago, you stated that you were certain that, although it might take 20 or 30 years, Tibet would regain her freedom. Do you still believe this? Under what conditions do you feel this liberation will take place?

A. Certainly! I now believe it more strongly than ever. Of course, it would be difficult to say exactly how liberation will come about. The determination of the Tibetan people inside and outside Tibet is the main basis of our hope; but the fact that China has been having continual internal problems, particularly within Tibet—economic, social and political problems—is equally encouraging in terms of Tibet's potential for regaining her rights.

   The Tibetan issue has, since 1959, been an extremely sensitive topic for the Chinese. They are always alert to any mention of Tibet. This proves their lack of confidence in their control.

Q. What sort of political and social policies would you advocate in the event of your return to Tibet?

A. In the early Sixties a draft of the basic policies of the Tibetan Government was drawn up, but of course these are only tentative. Policies must be established in accordance with the will of the majority of the people, which in the case of Tibet means those who have remained in Tibet throughout the Chinese occupation.

Q. How difficult will it be to restore the country's religion, culture and way of life?

A. Restoring the religion will be extremely difficult but, anyway, religion is the business of the individual. As for the culture, this will require much thought.

   In the old tradition, religion and politics were combined. Here, the word 'politics' does not have the same connotation as it does in the West. It just means the managing of temporal, or worldly activities. In theory, 'temporal' implies activities which bring eternal benefit. In other words, 'temporal' implies the maintaining of a decent standard of living and 'religion' implies the development of

126

the mind. Since all human beings have both a body and a mind, it is theoretically ideal for these two activities to be combined.

In many countries a great deal of material progress has been made, yet the people of these countries still experience various forms of mental suffering. On the other hand, if a country is spiritually developed but has a poor material standard, like India for example, its people experience physical sufferings such as disease, hunger and so forth. If temporal and religious activities can be integrated within a governmental system it is certainly very good. Therefore, it is my belief that, in order for a system to be truly effective, its leader must be either a saint or a philosopher.

In Tibet this unification of temporal and religious affairs was attempted. As with all social systems, it had its shortcomings. On the one hand, the standard of living was not always satisfactory, and on the other hand, spiritual leaders sometimes became excessively involved in politics, thus directly or indirectly harming the purity of religion. When we return to Tibet we shall have to give a great deal of thought to this problem and act in accordance with the developments current at the time.

National economic theories are far too complicated to be discussed here, but in short it can be said that if a state wishes to claim that all its citizens are equal then it must ensure that each of them has an equal economic status. If there is not equality of wealth then individual rights cannot exist in practice. A poor man can never compete with a rich man. Maintaining this equality is a delicate problem. It would be wonderful if this could be left to the integrity of the individual, just as a Buddhist monk is responsible for his own religious practice; but such a policy would never work. Here perhaps socialism has something to offer. Unfortunately, no ideological system is perfect; each has its good and bad points. In Tibet's case, we shall have to adopt policies suited to the unique nature of the country's geography, to the mentality of her people, and to her current circumstances.

Politically, the present world atmosphere is not at all good, not at all healthy. It seems that attachment and hatred predominate in every system. If we were to copy these politics it would neither be possible to combine politics and religion nor would it be of benefit to the Tibetan people.

Politics should be an instrument to serve society but these days this sometimes seems to be reversed.

2. POLITICAL THEORIES

Q. It is a common belief that political and spiritual activities are mutually contradictory, yet the lineage of Dalai Lamas is an obvious exception to this. Does the answer to this lie within the form of Buddhism practised by the Dalai Lamas and, if so, in what way?

A. In Tibet, the entire government, involving thousands of people, was based on this combination system. Perhaps such a system, which would have been more difficult in many other places, was feasible in Tibet because its religion is Mahayana Buddhism, which places such strong emphasis on benefitting beings, and thus on the fulfilling of the needs of society. Our system had faults, yet I believe that these aren't to be blamed on Mahayana Buddhism but on the social structure.

Q. Many political scientists assert that a religious government is not workable in an industrial society. What are your views on this?

A. I don't think that it is any more difficult to have this kind of government in an industrial than in an agriculturally-based society. Religion is entirely a mental attitude. It has nothing to do, essentially, with the physical activities that may surround it.

Q. What does Your Holiness think of the use of violence, such as guerilla activities and sabotage, as a political tactic?

A. Violence is never good, and in the circumstances particular to Tibet it is impractical and ineffective.

3. TIBET AND CHINA'S PAST RELATIONS

Q. China claims that for many centuries she has enjoyed sovereignty over Tibet. Yet Tibet has never recognised this sovereignty and, in actual fact, lived in seeming independence. How does Your Holiness interpret the historical relationship of the two countries?

A. From the religious point of view, the Tibetans always considered that the relationship was one of guru and patron. For centuries the court of China looked to the high lamas of Tibet for spiritual leadership, and in return Tibetan lamas frequently visited China to teach.

Politically, even as early as the time of the Great Kings of Tibet (6th to 8th centuries) the status of the two countries was equal. On one occasion, Tibet even invaded China and the Emperor had to flee for his life.

However, history always speaks in terms of past tense, whereas what counts is the present reality. If, right now, the Tibetan people are happy under the Chinese occupation and the majority of the Tibetan people are satisfied and agree to remain under Chinese domination, then there is no problem. Whether in the past Tibet was independent or not would be irrelevant. But the actual situation is such that Tibetans are not in the least bit content with the Chinese occupation, culturally or materially. Since 1959 the Chinese have had a completely free hand in all activities in Tibet. They could have done anything they wished. By now, they should have at least been able to raise the standard of living of the people, but even this has not happened.

4. LIFE IN EXILE

Q. At this point in time, does His Holiness still consider his government-in-exile to be the sole legal representative of the people of Tibet?

A. (Laughter) We needn't bother too much about legal or illegal. Sometimes even if you are legal you might become illegal and if illegal you might want to become legal. What counts is that the majority of Tibetans are placing their hopes here, in this government. Because of this we have a tremendous responsibility. This is the darkest age in Tibet's 2,100 year old history. I consider it a great honour and privilege to be carrying the responsibility that my position entails.

Q. What are the functions of the government-in-exile and what has it achieved?

A. The government here is formed of various departments run by members who, largely, have been elected by the refugees. These departmental heads are consulted on any major issues that arise. They must carry out the functions of their offices and maintain a liaison with the people.

In refugee work, the principal tasks are educating the young and settling the adults. Our main responsibility, however, is the greater task of regaining the rights of the Tibetan nation, and for this all that can be done, under the circumstances, is being done.

Q. You have now spent exactly half your life outside Tibet. Are you tired of living in exile?

A. No, I have learned many things from living as a refugee. It has helped my spiritual practice. In a desperate situation one cannot pretend everything is all right. One must accept reality. Now the Dalai Lama is more realistic. When I was in Tibet, the Dalai Lama was something really big and important. Despite my own efforts to make contact with the common people, sometimes it was difficult. Now there is much more contact with the common people. Also, there is a Tibetan saying: "When you become a monk, any place that is habitable becomes your country." So whether I am in Tibet or India or America or Europe, it does not make very much difference—except for the climate. Sometimes it is very hot.

Q. Like other refugee communities, the preservation of your culture must be an ever-present concern. Can Tibetan culture persevere among the new generation growing up in India who have never seen their homeland? How do you overcome the pressures of assimilation into another culture?

A. From the start, the exiled community was concerned about preserving Tibetan culture and identity. In India and elsewhere we refugees try to maintain our settlements in such a way as to preserve Tibetan traditions.

Take education, for example. With (former Prime Minister) Nehru's help, blessings and financial support, we established separate Tibetan schools so that students could study Tibetan language and history.

(In Dharamsala), we have a central administration that maintains excellent communications among Tibetans, not only in India but also abroad. By maintaining close contacts, we help to preserve our identity.

In other countries, more people are showing interest in Tibetan traditions and Tibetan Buddhism. That, I think, helps young Tibetan exiles. Once, they might have simply forgotten about being Tibetan. Now they see, from the example of foreigners, that our ways have value. We lost our country, it's true. But that was not due to internal causes, but to external aggression.

I always tell these young Tibetans: "You are Tibetan, whether you live in America or anywhere else. No matter how hard you try, you cannot turn Western 100 percent. If you forget about your own culture completely, the final result is that you will be neither Tibetan nor Western. It is far better, simply in your own interest, to maintain Tibetan ways."

Q. Although you tell young Tibetans to maintain their identity, they must be learning new things from being in technologically advanced countries. Do you think this abrupt confrontation with modernity will have a positive effect if you go back to Tibet?

A. Oh yes, no doubt. We have to change our old way of life. In Tibet, there was much backwardness. We must catch up with the world and develop as a modern nation. But I firmly believe in the combination of material progress with mental progress. These two elements must go together. Without either one, we may not achieve satisfactory happiness.

Q. The Tibetan people here in India are refugees. They are poor and yet, looking at them, they seem so happy. What is the secret?

A. I don't know. You can't find anything, yet there is something. I believe one factor is just what I was saying: their tradition is based on a realisation of the importance of human life or human rights. Tibetan people regard life, any life, as something very sacred, something holy and important, so even when a small insect is killed, we immediately respond with some feeling of compassion. This remains a force in our society. We are usually happy and good-hearted in our whole community. Of course, there is occasional fighting, even killing. But generally there is harmony and good feeling, mainly due to the teaching of Mahayana Buddhism—the very great emphasis on the importance of kindness and tolerance, love and compassion.

Q. Do you believe that refugee Tibetans may someday return to Tibet?

A. It's possible. I strongly believe that. So long as human determination is there, things will change. Inside Tibet nationalism is even stronger than among those in exile. Quite remarkably, the Tibetan people's determination is stronger than the Dalai Lama's determination.

The real factor which makes for this determination is the Chinese. The Chinese made the Tibetans tough and determined. Moreover, they brought out the greatness of Tibetan strength, will-power and unity. So from that point of view, we must be grateful to the Chinese! (Laughs.)

Q. If you could address all of the Tibetan people, what message would you deliver?

A. Get a good education and be honest.

5. TIBET TODAY

Q. Does Your Holiness receive reliable information on what is going on inside Tibet today?

A. Certainly. This we consider to be absolutely mandatory. Here, we must act in accordance with the wishes of the Tibetan people who are in Tibet, and so we must know what they are thinking.

Q. Are there any guerilla groups still fighting the Chinese within Tibet?

A. It is very difficult for large, organised guerilla forces to exist, but throughout Tibet there have been revolts from time to time out of desperation.

Q. How many Chinese are in Tibet today and, of these, how many are soldiers?

A. This is also difficult to say for certain. I would estimate that there are approximately a third of a million soldiers there. Just prior to the Lhasa Revolt of 1959 there were more than 120,000. Maintaining control of Tibet is requiring about two and a half times that number. On top of this, approximately 100,000 Chinese civilians have been brought in.

Q. Escaping refugees have given reports of Tibetan women being forced to marry Chinese soldiers and Tibetan children being forcibly separated from their parents and sent to China for 'education', the former to destroy Tibet as a blood race and the latter to destroy it as a culture. What has been the outcome of these activities?

A. Both of these have failed. Most of the forced marriages have now been dissolved and the project has largely been abandoned.

As for the children taken to China, most of them eventually return to Tibet to work in various fields. At the beginning they have great determination and enthusiasm, but gradually they turn anti-Chinese. When they are in China they hear only Chinese talk—progress, development, happiness and so forth—but when they return to Tibet they see what is really happening. They become disenchanted and usually become key-persons in leading the resistance. Some get arrested, but most use their training to subtly work against the Chinese, making it difficult for the Chinese to capture them. They use the very education they received from the Chinese to resist the Chinese, and so from the Chinese point of view the tactic has completely backfired. From our point of view it has been very successful.

Q. What language is used in the educational and governmental systems?

A. In government offices, Chinese is spoken almost exclusively. In schools Chinese is the medium in which most subjects are taught. Here the Chinese have adopted a rather cunning approach. Tibetan is taught, but if anyone shows more interest in Chinese their prospects become far greater and they meet with no hindrances. In addition to this, the standard of education is very low, the main emphasis being on Mao's thought. Most schools are more like labour camps than educational institutions.

Q. The Chinese say they have improved the economic and educational facilities in Tibet. Is there any truth in this claim?

A. As for education, they have established more schools. Before 1959 there were very few institutions, and modern education was virtually non-existent. Since the Chinese came, they did open many schools.

But we have to evaluate this issue from a wider perspective. First of all, the real standard of education is very low. It is, in reality, a child labour camp. They have a short study period, and the rest of the time they are used as field workers. Since 1979 (which marked the implementation of general liberalisation in China), education has seen some improvement, but the standard is still very low.

There was no modern education in old Tibet, but many monasteries acted as learning centres. All of that has been completely destroyed by the Chinese.

Economic production has been increased, no question. But all of the production is rigidly controlled. Most of the products are taken away to China, and the real amount consumed by Tibetans is very little. There is strict rationing, and the people's stomachs are often empty.

Q. You have said that the religious fervour of young Tibetans these days is even stronger than that of their elders. Why is that?

A. The Chinese have suppressed religious activities so much that the result has been counterproductive. Even the older Tibetans are surprised at the degree of religious faith. There is not a single outstanding communist among today's Tibetan youth. Of the older Tibetans who joined the Communist Party in the 1930s and '40s, nearly all have been disgraced. The young Tibetan communists are uneducated, simple-minded sycophants. Some can't even read Tibetan. Naturally the people don't respect them and call them 'helicopters' because they are promoted so quickly.

133

6. RELATIONS BETWEEN INDIA AND TIBET

Q. Does India need a Tibetan buffer-zone?

A. I cannot answer this question definitely. I don't represent the Indian government or the Indian people. However, generally speaking, the relationship between India and Tibet is something that is very close historically and culturally. Buddhism came to Tibet from India, and with Buddhism came a great flow of Indian culture. In a cultural sense we Tibetans are students of India; they are our guru, we their disciple. From that viewpoint we are historically close. Tibetans have been travelling to the Buddhist places of pilgrimage in India for centuries, despite the great distance and the hard and perilous conditions. Similarly, many Indians have frequented places of pilgrimage in Tibet, such as Mount Kailash, Lake Mansarovar and so forth. Despite the tremendous cold, thousands of Indian friends have continued to visit these Tibetan holy sites. So our cultural relationship was very close. On top of this Tibet's geographical border is enormous and is located in rugged Himalayan mountains. Any political problem in Tibet therefore naturally becomes a problem to India. From that perspective Tibet is very significant to India.

7. BUDDHISM AND MARXISM

Q. You often say that you are not against communism and find some good things in it. Could you please explain what you mean by this statement?

A. If there were no good points in communism, there would be no reason for the attraction of so many people towards it. Of course, there are many defects in terms of practical application.

One of the main reasons why I respect communism is that basically it is concerned with the majority, the lower class, the working man. Secondly, everybody needs something, but the need of the lower class is urgent, a question of life and death. So here is a theory which is more concerned with the poor majority, those who are in urgent need. This is very good. The communist theory calculates on the basis of producer and consumer, and is against the masses producing and a small group consuming. So I feel that here the point they raise is valid.

In reality, unless there is economic equality, social and political equality is very difficult to achieve. I am not criticising other systems and nations; I have no right to criticise. I firmly believe that each nation has a right to practise its own ideas. That's very important. So I am not criticising others. But in many so-called democratic countries, the rich people always get the top places. There is equality in the constitution but due to a poor economic situation the poor cannot reach the political top.

Of course it would be ideal if everybody voluntarily dedicated themselves to the community, like the former Prime Minister Desai appealing to the Indian landlords to give up their surplus land. To some extent there were very good results. But still, all beings are not pure. Unless there is some pressure, some people won't listen. This is the difficulty. If under such circumstances there is an organisation which creates equality for everybody, I think it is good. But I am mainly referring to the original Marxism, not the practices in the present systems and nations. Here I myself sometimes get confused: China is claiming that Russia is not truly Marxist; Russia points out the same to Peking. So who is truly Marxist? I don't know. It is difficult to say. And now with the growth of European communism we also have French, Italian and Spanish communist systems.

Q. You have said that there are many similarities between Buddhism and Marxism. Could you tell us what are the most important differences?

A. Buddhism emphasises not only this life, but the long future. There is not an emphasis on material progress. Buddhism concerns all sentient beings.

Marxism is concerned with only this life, and only materialism, only human beings, and only the working class. And within that, only party members, and within that, high-ranking ones. [Laughs]

[In saying the two philosophies are similar] I refer to original Marxism. The present Marxism is interpreted according to the Chinese or the Soviet Union. Those states are not practising Marxism purely. It is simply mixed with nationalism and power politics. Otherwise there is no reason to fight between China and the Soviet Union or between China and Vietnam. Marxism is talking about the less privileged human beings, the working class, the needy people. That's absolutely right. Between them there is no national boundary. From that viewpoint, there is no single reason to fight with socialist brothers and sisters.

8. LIBERATION AND TERRORISM

Q. In a world in which so-called liberation groups that employ violent tactics for their ends proliferate, the Tibetan freedom movement remains distinct in that it adheres to non-violence. Would you say that this is due to the pervasiveness of Buddhism in Tibetan culture? In general, how does Buddhism address such issues as nationalism, terrorism and liberation?

A. I think the Buddhist viewpoint is that liberation means any action for greater happiness for the people concerned. The main purpose of the Buddha's teachings is for temporary benefit as well as long-term benefit. The long-term benefit is nirvana, Buddhahood or enlightenment. Temporary benefit is a happy life.

In terms of Tibetan liberation, or the Tibetan question, the Chinese brought fear, suspicion and the destruction of human relationships. I think this is the worst kind of oppression.

Though the old (Tibetan) society had many defects, overall it produced a decent person. You can still see that among our exiled community in India. Generally speaking, Tibetans are jovial, gentle and honest. That kind of human community was produced by the old society.

If the society is completely wrong, as the Chinese say, then how is it possible to produce such a nice, decent community? In any case, that society's structure is completely destroyed in Tibet now. But the Chinese utterly failed to introduce a new meaningful society. That's their greatest failure.

I think there are similar problems in the Soviet Union, and in Mongolia. Their systems are far too centralised, and the people on top are often ignorant. Their systems are marked by fear and suspicion. In a free society, even when the government fails there are still individuals who create new ideas and institutions, so that human evolution may continue. In the Chinese model, the normal evolutionary process stops and all innovation comes down from the top.

As for a Buddhist perspective on terrorism, we believe that violence is wrong. Through violence, it is possible to gain something. But I feel such gains are only temporary. You may solve one problem but in the long-run you will create another problem. We see this in the conflict between the Israelis and the Arabs. The best way is through non-violence. It may take time, but once you've solved the problem, it's once and for all.

9. Present Relations With China

Q. Is it true that the People's Republic of China has recently invited you to return to Tibet? If so, under what conditions could you accept such an invitation?

A. We Tibetans became refugees because of political reasons and not because we committed crimes in Tibet. The situation in Tibet was exceedingly hard and we felt we could do more by leaving. In the 20 years since this decision was made we have done a great deal in the field of preservation of Tibetan culture and the Tibetan identity. Tibetan culture has two aspects: the social culture of the nation; and the culture that revolved around the philosophical issues aimed at understanding basic human sufferings, such as birth, sickness, old age and death. We feel that as long as there is human suffering this aspect of our culture should be preserved, for this culture is very useful and effective in bringing happiness to the minds of people. As for aspects of Tibetan culture that are not beneficial to man, things that are just leftovers from the past, it is sufficient to preserve a record of these in books. It would not be possible to preserve a living tradition of these things, and there would be no value in attempting to do so. But the Buddhist aspect of the culture is very valuable.

Living as refugees in India we have done much more to preserve this than we could possibly have done from inside (Tibet). I feel that until the time comes when the majority of Tibetans in Tibet are genuinely satisfied and truthfully made happy, I can best serve my country and my people from the outside and as a refugee.

Q. How do you deal with the subject of violence, such as the Chinese taking Tibet?

A. Violence is very bad. Generally speaking, through violence, even though you may get some temporary benefit it will create another problem. It is not a proper method.

In the Tibetan case, for the last 20 years the Chinese followed a very suppressive attitude, just killing, just bullets. They completely failed. Not only in Tibet, but in China proper. Failed. So they are compelled to follow more moderate policies. This short history itself proves that violence is not successful.

Q. But over a period of time, how much patience does one require?

A. Patience, I think, has different interpretations. In the sense of not increasing a feeling of hatred, one must have infinite patience. But some people get the impression that patience means passivity, that when some incident happens one should not react. If someone does something bad one should take countermeasures, that is very necessary, but without losing mental peace. So mentally, one is still in the position of patience. But in action, one takes countermeasures.

Q. Do you see some hopeful change in China?
A. There are good signs, but it is still too early to tell. I read in a newspaper that in China even the past is not certain. [Laughter]

Q. Can the present Chinese government co-exist with a Buddhist Tibet?
A. At present, Chinese communism, I don't think so. They are very much ignorant, very much ignorant. In the communist belief, religion is opium. But some Chinese scholars indicated that this does not include Buddhism.

Q. Is that because it is a godless religion?
A. I don't know the exact meaning. According to some Western Buddhist scholars, Buddhism is not religion. Buddhism is a science of mind.

Q. Is Western science a religion?
A. Yes. Communism also has become a religion, in a wider perspective.

Q. When you meet with Chinese officials, how will you express your feelings about the situation in Tibet?
A. I will simply argue that the six million Tibetans should be treated as human beings. The Chinese came to Tibet not as aggressors but as 'liberators'. As liberators, they should have brought benefits for the Tibetan people. Instead they brought new suffering and destruction. Most of the monasteries have been totally destroyed. If for 30 years the Chinese had adopted a truly friendly attitude, then today the majority of Tibetans would say, "Okay, I'm very happy." But that is not the case. Fortunately the Chinese have realised their past mistakes. Even so, every mistake is still blamed on the 'Gang of Four'— even destruction that occurred before the Gang of Four. That is rather silly.

Q. Are you optimistic that conditions will continue to improve?
A. In general I'm optimistic. Optimism is better than pessimism.

Q. If Deng Xiaoping were in this room right now, what would you say to him?

A. I would advise him to study Tibetan history and culture. A true Marxist must be scientific, not simply an echo of Marxist dogma. To be scientific one must be realistic.

10. SCIENCE

Q. We were told that you are interested in the workings of the mind from a scientific point of view. May we ask what is your specific interest?

A. My personal interest is consciousness, how to function. In Buddhism there are many categories within mind, or consciousness. There are hundreds of distinctions. According to modern science, they say the mind has more than 12 billion cells. Within that, up to now only a few hundred [are understood]. The rest of them are still in mystery.

It is very interesting to know modern scientific findings and our own Buddhist explanations. In the Buddhist teaching there are levels of consciousness. There are also varieties of dreams and visions. The deepest consciousness experience occurs when we are dying.

Q. Who will you speak to here about this?

A. I don't know. Anyone who knows. [Laughs] For example, last year in Austria there was a seminar on Eastern Wisdom and Western Science. Among the participants were some neurologists and physicists. I visited a famous nuclear research centre in Switzerland. There I met some physicists, they explained quantum theory and quarks—these things. About the quantum theory, still I'm very much confused. I'm very keen to learn these things.

The physicist's subject is not consciousness, but phenomena, the smallest particles. They are always changing, interdependent, according to the theory of relativity. In Buddhist philosophy this is a very important subject, interdependence.

There also is the 'Big Bang' theory, one which was explained very forcefully. Twelve billion years ago was the exact time of the big bang!

Q. What do you think?

A. I don't know! [Laughs]

Q. What is your theory of the beginning of the universe?

A. I am Buddhist. So you see....that's an explanation. One thing is quite similar between the scientific explanation and the Buddhist explanation—that through the four elements, heat, liquid, air, earth, on the basis of space, somehow due to their moving the whole universe is formed, all the galaxies. Then they degenerate and disappear, and are formed again. Astronomers have found already 10 billion galaxies.

11. THE ROLE OF THE DALAI LAMA

Q. You have said that among the changes you'd like to implement in a free Tibet is a democratic political system. Wouldn't such an elected leadership threaten to usurp your position as leader of the Tibetan people?

A. I believe in democratic leadership. In our national constitution (drafted by the Tibetan government-in-exile in Dharamsala in 1963), it stipulates that, according to majority opinion, even the Dalai Lama's position could be changed.

Sometimes I feel that when we go back to Tibet and things become normal, I will follow Mahatma Gandhi's example. He was a freedom fighter, but once India attained its independence he did not lead the country...

The Dalai Lama would retire and remain a humble monk, watching the situation. Other people would carry the responsibility. If something becomes seriously wrong, then I could intervene. Otherwise, I'd have time to relax. (Laughs)

In the future, we want to have a united Tibet—including what the Chinese designate the Tibetan Autonomous Region and areas of eastern Tibet which have been absorbed into Chinese provinces, such as Sichuan and Yunnan—with a firm central authority. In such a structure, the presence of a figure with no real power but with wide popularity could be most helpful.

Q. Your symbolic role among Tibetans has been likened to the role of the present Pope for the Polish people. Would you comment on this analogy?

A. There are great similarities. But in the case of Tibet and the Dalai Lama, it is not only the present generation which is concerned. The relationship goes back for centuries.

In this sense, it is much deeper than the relationship between the present Pope and the Polish people. On the other hand, the papal institution is worldwide, a recognised and independent institution. The Dalai Lama is just a refugee. (Laughs)

Q. If something should happen to you and your life is lost between now and the time you go back, a search for another Dalai Lama will take place. Is it possible that that search will take place outside of Tibet?
A. Absolutely.

Q. How would this happen?
A. That's not my decision. Let other people do it. The Dalai Lama as an institution may still be a useful thing. If they wish to keep that, they'll not face any problem in finding another one.

Q. In an article published in a Dutch periodical Your Holiness stated that you may be the last in the line of Dalai Lamas. Is this true, and what does it mean?
A. (Laughter) Maybe the last, I don't know. Anyway, beings possessing the qualifications to be Dalai Lama are always there. The incarnation of a Buddha or Bodhisattva always continues to manifest, not only in human form but sometimes as an insect, as an animal and so forth. Whether or not a particular being is given the title of 'Dalai Lama' depends on whether or not such a process is beneficial. For example, long before the First Dalai Lama there were many other incarnations of the Bodhisattva Avalokitesvara, such as Drom Tonpa and Kunga Nying-po; but these were not given the title of 'Dalai Lama'. The title of Dalai Lama was actually first given to the Third Dalai Lama, Sonam Gyatso. They then traced back through two previous incarnations of this man to Gendun Drub, the disciple of Lama Je Tsong Khapa (founder of the Yellow Hat School), and called him and his successive incarnation the First and Second Dalai Lamas. Now, the First Dalai Lama, Gendun Drub, had clearly remembered his previous incarnation, which had been a Nepalese Lama by the name of Padma Dorje; but this previous incarnation was not given the title 'Dalai Lama'.

Anyway, I am not the best Dalai Lama, but also I am not the worst. Therefore it might be best to be the last.

Q. Many people would interpret the end of the line of Dalai Lamas to mean the end of Tibet as an independent nation.
A. Possibly, but this would be a wrong interpretation. I am far more

concerned with the Tibetan issue than with the office of Dalai Lama as such. This is the responsibility of being a Dalai Lama. As long as the title 'Dalai Lama' is useful for Tibet it will be continued. Should it become no longer useful, there would be little value in maintaining it. This is in reference to the Tibet question. On the other hand, I am also a Buddhist monk of the Mahayana tradition vowed to the uplifting of all sentient beings and according to this vow must actively work in the world, lifetime upon lifetime, until all beings gain enlightenment. This is the pledge of every Mahayana Buddhist. So I have these two responsibilities. As long as the title 'Dalai Lama' is an effective tool in fulfilling them, it will be maintained. Thus, perhaps I am the last Dalai Lama; but then again, perhaps not. If it is of greater benefit to beings for me to reincarnate as, for example, a dog or a bridge, then as a Mahayanist it is my duty to do so.